PALM ISLAND

Jason L. Bradshaw

Copyright ©

www.authorjasonlbradshaw.com

No part of this publication may be transmitted or reproduced in any form or by means, electronic, mechanical, photocopied, recorded, or otherwise, without the written permission of Jason L. Bradshaw or

Publishers Note: Palm Island is a work of fiction. Characters, names, places, and incidents are either the author's imagination or are used fictitiously, and any resemblance to an actual person, living or dead, business establishments, events, or locations is entirely coincidental.

This edition was published by arrangement of Jason L. Bradshaw

First Print

CHAPTER ONE

Daxton could hear the giant raindrops starting to hit the rusted-out tin roof of the bar. It started slowly but like all the showers in the islands, it could get intense pretty quickly. He used to be interested in the weather so he would check the radar and forecast frequently but he really didn't care anymore. It didn't matter to him whether it was dark and stormy or a sunny day with pleasant balmy breezes. It was in his blood back then. The weather, the winds, the waves, and the sea but he lost his passion for it long ago, the same as he'd lost the passion for most things in life. Now he was just holding down a bar stool in some washed-out island town trying to figure out what the hell brought him to this Moment in his life. He could feel the sweat building up on his eyebrow just before it dripped into his half-empty beer, and he thought to himself as he shook his head, "Jesus, Daxton, this is what it's like to be at rock bottom". He looked down at his hot stale beer as the compass that dangled around his neck swung into his view. It swung back and forth as he tried to maintain a half-assed vertical stance on the barstool.

He looked down with one eye at the TAG watch around his wrist. It was literally the only thing of value he still had to his name. His, kind of ex, Kelsey bought it for him as a gift and it was the only thing he gave a fuck about besides her and his daughter, Skyler. The watch told him that it was eight-thirty and he thought "Damn, I'm way too drunk for it to be this early". Daxton rapidly blinked his eyes thinking it might help clear his vision. It didn't.

The bartender, Bruce walked over to the end of the bar where Daxton was semi-standing next to the barstool. He threw the rag he had been using to mop up the bar in front of Daxton saying "Let me guess, put it on your tab, right Bruh? You do understand this runs out sooner or later Daxton?"

He could hear Bruce talking but he was too drunk to give two shits about responding at that point. It was like Bruce's voice was reverberating in his head, almost like Charlie Brown's teacher speaking to her class. He could see the flashes of lightning, but he couldn't hear the thunder anymore. He hadn't had water in weeks, probably hadn't eaten in four days, and hadn't had a shower in probably longer but Daxton didn't care. All he cared about now was what had dropped into his lap that morning.

Earlier in the day he sat there at the bar and studied the two coordinates that were written on a small piece of paper and couldn't help but wonder. "Why me? Why the fuck would anyone hire me to run them over there? And why the hell would they pay so much to a washed-up half-assed captain?"

Things weren't adding up, but he knew if he wanted to afford Skyler's last year of college, he really didn't have a choice. He was flat-ass broke, at the end of his credit and there were no other options on the table for him. He figured no one would welcome him or even care if he disappeared forever at that point. This island, just like from where he came was completely done with him, apart from a few people who had befriended him and wanted to help him.

Daxton knew that this was something he had to do. Like it or not, this was going to be the next and biggest chapter in his life. It was time to turn the page.

About the time he felt himself sway just a little far-off kilter, he felt a familiar hand rub over his right shoulder. He slowly turned his head and tried to focus out of his left eye.

"Hey there, you handsome devil, you doing okay tonight?" Kalea stood next to Daxton bracing his shoulder to keep him from falling over. Daxton smirked and slung his arm over Kalea's neck and tried to form the words as best he could.

"Aww, there she is, my sweet, sweet Kalea" Daxton threw his hand up into the air and pointed at the bartender. "Bruce! Get this gorgeous young lady a drink stat! Put it on my tab!"

Kalea looked at Bruce and shook her head no and winked at Bruce. "I tell you what Dax, let's go back to your place and have a nightcap. No need to drink out here. Bruce overcharges you anyways" She kissed him on the cheek as he swayed in place for a few Moments, and he realized that was probably the best bet for him. He knew he needed to get his act together.

It was time that he needed to put some real thought into this new opportunity he had been approached with. Kalea pulled him off his barstool and motioned to Bruce that she was taking him home. This was a common exercise with Daxton, Kalea, and Bruce. "Good night you guys" Bruce yelled as they walked down the caliche walkway.

Daxton woke up that Tuesday morning totally clothed and smelling like a hobo in the hot sun. He ran his hands across his unshaven sunburnt face as he tried to swallow and reach for his wallet. The dream he had was the same reoccurring dream he'd had since the plane crash. He couldn't shake it. The crash, the explosions, the screaming, the smells, and the way he'd handled it afterward. "I put that plane exactly where I should have and still lost people's lives."

He found his beat-up leather wallet and opened the note again that had the coordinates written on it as Kalea once again reached upon his shoulder. "Hey Dax, how are you feeling this morning?"

Daxton turned around as Kalea lay naked in his bed. The sun was shining in the broken window making her face glow. Daxton couldn't help but smile and admire her stunning beauty.

He threw down his wallet and note on the nightstand and wrapped Kalea up in a giant embrace. She nestled into his arms and laid her head on his chest and took a deep breath. Dax looked down at her and ran his fingers through her hair. "What is it girl, what is bothering you?" She reached up and rubbed his compass that hung from his necklace between her thumb and index finger. "What happened to you along your journey Dax, did she break your heart that bad? I know there is so much good, so much love in you but you destroy yourself every single day and night." Daxton laid his head back and looked at the slow-turning ceiling fan. Kalea sat up and straddled Daxton looking him in the eye. "I have loved you since you stepped foot onto this Island Daxton Shaw, as these others laugh at you now, I only see a broken soul and heart. The things you have done, the things you have seen, and the love that you have experienced. I can only imagine what you struggle with each and every day. And I continue to come to your side because I know of the greatness you possess."

CHAPTER TWO

Daxton Shaw grew up in the small bayside community of Rockport, Texas. It was a little salty town where everyone knew each other, and the local kids could never get away with anything without Mother Karens alerting the entire town.

He grew up close to his cousins and played on the football team until his Junior year when he really fell in love with being on the water. It was his outlet and his safe place. He was on a boat with his family or friends since he had been in diapers. By the time he was 16, he was so familiar with the bay system and the weather that even the local guides would call him to ask him questions and get updates. Even though he got into some minor typical teenage trouble he was a good kid. Helped his neighbors, and his teachers and even stayed behind once to help the community after a large hurricane came ashore in their town.

Daxton's family was middle-class and although college was an option his parents gave him, he knew it just wasn't for him. He graduated from the town's small high school in 1996 but just barely. He had missed so many days of his senior year they wanted to keep him another full year. When he walked in to sign himself out for good his counselor decided to do what she could to help him walk the stage and get on with his life. She knew that Daxton had his sights set on the Marine Corps and she hated to see him unable to follow his dream to serve his country. Daxton had outgrown the small-town life. It wasn't that he didn't love the town or his friends and family he just wanted more, wanted to see the world and then settle down somewhere other than the town where he had spent his entire young life

He kept in touch with his cousin who had joined the Air Force after he graduated from high school and was totally enthralled with the stories of travel and the fun he was having while he served.

After graduation, Daxton joined the Marine Corps and reported to the Marine Corps Air Station, Cherry Point North Carolina. His superiors were impressed with him across the board. He was eager to learn, determined to succeed, and very athletic. He was born to be a Marine and to serve his country proudly.

Less than a year after he graduated, he was briskly shipped to Afghanistan where he would spend the next two years of his life working in some of the most volatile regions. His kind heart and humor made him a celebrity in the local villages with the children and families that wanted noting to do with the conflict.

CHAPTER THREE

Daxton walked into the old, dilapidated hangar and went straight to the fridge. The refrigerator door was almost rusted through, and it made some horrible noises, but it did keep the beer cold. His phone rang and he pulled it out of his pocket and looked down at the cracked screen. A photo of a woman appeared on the screen as the phone rang. "Screw that, not today devil woman." He mumbled under his breath as he slid the phone back into his tore up jeans pocket. He pulled a cold Modelo out of the fridge and headed over toward the workbench. He grabbed a small toolbox and sat on his barstool when his voicemail inbox went off.

He squinted his eyes for a Moment. She never leaves a message, he thought to himself. He stood up pulled his phone out of his pocket again and hit okay. "Hey Daxton, it's me. Please give me a call when you can. We need to talk. I know things have been rough for you lately, but Liam has a pretty good opportunity that I think might help you out. Anyways, just call me when you can. Talk to you then...." Daxton listened to the message twice and contemplated just deleting it. He swiped his finger slowly over the delete button and then just threw his phone up on the workbench. If she had mentioned Skyler, he would have called back instantly but he didn't have any interest anymore in her or what Liam had to offer. He wasn't a big fan of Liam's, but he didn't have to deal with him, and he was no threat to Skyler, so he just let it all roll along.

He sat back down on his barstool again pulled over the oily Yamaha outboard carburetor and took four slugs off his Modelo. Just about that time, Brad came through the hangar door. "I was surprised to see your jeep sitting out there this early after last night or did you just come to sleep here?" Daxton wadded up a shop rag, turned around, and threw it at Brad.

Brad dodged it as it flew toward his head. "Easy killer! Just jacking with you buddy."

Daxton shook his head. "For the record, I did not sleep here. Not last night anyways. The time I did that the mosquitoes obviously found their way in, pretty sure I got malaria or Hep and lost about a half gallon of blood that night!"

Brad laughed and walked to the refrigerator as he looked at his watch. "Got any more beer in here? I don't have to do shit for the next three days and the wife is headed up to Mexico City to spend some time with her bitch of a sister."

Daxton swirled his fingers in the air telling Brad, "Make it two, I brought a case from the house and I'm in the same boat. Except for the whole wife part. No charters of flights for the next few days."

Brad was also a pilot years ago but gave up flying after he found out his eyesight was failing. He enjoyed being on the water much more than flying anyway so it had worked out for him. He had traveled to the area for years on fishing trips and on one of his visits, he fell in love with a beautiful local.

He moved full time to the region shorty after, they married and had two children. His wife was an English teacher and Brad worked as a freelance captain filling in for others in the area. He also owned two dive boats that he managed and personally operated from time to time. Brad was one of the first people that Daxton met when he moved to the islands. They shared many passions and hit it off almost immediately. Brad knew there were trauma issues in Daxton's past but didn't pry into his friend's past. Daxton appreciated that and they spent many hours on the water and holding up barstools together for the past two years. Brad was a positive influence in Daxton's life and always tried to cheer him up or drag him from the darkness when he could.

"Right on man, you getting any busier on your flights these days? You seem to be flying a little more often."

Daxton pulled off the bottom portion of the carburetor. "Ehh, maybe a little. AV gas went down and so did the flight prices.

I think the owner is charging less so it helps. He's not paying me shit so I'm sure he can charge less. But it gets me up in the air so it's all good."

"Good to hear, how are you and Kalea doing these days?"

Daxton drank the rest of his Modelo and opened his new one before he spoke. "It's complicated, I feel bad for her honestly. Same shit every day. Daxon has too much to drink, Kalea thinks she has to baby sit and we redo it over and over. Don't get me wrong, we have some great times and she's such a great woman, but she needs something else. Someone better than me. Honestly Brad I think it's just a convenience kinda thing, I am just not feeling it, and I'm not sure if I have it in me anymore to be in a real relationship.

"Cheers to that dude, wouldn't take much of a man to be better than you, at least better looking anyways." The two of them clanked their beers together and chuckled.

"So, what's next on Daxton's to-do list then? Heading back to the states to see your daughter anytime soon?" Brad asked.

"Yeah, I'm planning on going up maybe next month if she gets a break from school and work. I miss her so much, but she is killing me these days being out and on her own. As far as a to-do list, hell I have no idea. My ex-ish wife left me a message earlier and said her man, slash fiancé' had some sort of opportunity for me. The thought makes me fucking cringe doing anything for that sleazeball but having extra funds would be nice.

I'm drowning and need to finish paying for Skyler's next tuition. Plus, the boss man is selling his plane and wants to give me the first shot at picking it up. He has no interest in flying charters down the other direction so he said I could go direct with those customers. Shit, who knows Brad. I'm a mess and change my mind daily. Just trying to get through a day at a time my friend."

Brad walked over and put his hand on Daxton's shoulder.

"You're a great father and a half-assed friend, you'll figure it all out. I have faith in you buddy, I will never ask you what happened but if you ever want to talk about it at all, know I'm always here."

"I appreciate that and one day we will have that conversation,

But for now, we take a tequila shot to start our time off."

Brad shook his head as Daxton opened the lower cabinet door and pulled out a bottle of Hornitos and two shot glasses. He poured the shots and handed one to Brad. Daxton raised his glass. "To strong winds and mermaids!" Brad lifted his shot into the air and they both tilted the glasses back and poured the shots into their mouths. They turned the shot glasses upside down and slammed the glasses on the workbench at the same time.

"Whooo, that was just as good as last night." Daxton wiped his mouth with his sleeve as his phone started to ring. He reached into his back pocket and pulled out his phone. A photo of Skyler appeared on the screen and Daxton's eyes lit up. "Hold that thought dude and we'll jump back into this here in just a bit, it's Sky."

CHAPTER FOUR

\Kelsey James was born and raised in a small town just outside Hot Springs, Arkansas. She had a very petite, athletic build, dark brown hair, a light olive complexion, and big gorgeous green eyes. She carried herself with confidence and pride. She was very well-spoken and well-traveled. Her parents, both doctors, owned the local family practice. Because Kelsey spent so much time at their offices, she grew up knowing practically everyone who resided in the little city. Her parents were a little older, as they had waited to start a family, but being more established meant they had a little more money than most. With that came travel for Kelsey. Her parents would take vacations four or five times a year and never to the same place. By the time she was ten, she had more stamps on her passport than ninety percent of adults. She knew how to scuba dive, ski, and surf by the time she entered high school. Learning was extremely easy for her, so she excelled at most subjects, and she was an excellent volleyball player, making Varsity her sophomore year. She was in the National Honor Society, captain of the volleyball team, and stayed involved in numerous events and festivities in and out of school. She was extremely active and busy like both of her parents. During her last year of high school, she took college electives to get a head start.

The medical field intrigued her, so she decided she wanted to pursue a career as a nurse. Before she sent applications for college, she decided she would rather enlist in the Air Force to get her nurse training while traveling and experiencing new things. Her dad was all for it as he had spent four years doing the same thing in the Navy. Her mother was not so keen on Kelsey's plan, but she knew that once an idea was in Kelsey's head, she was going to do what she wanted to do.

She aced the mental and physical testing and graduated at the top of her Air Force class. After three years of being bounced around parts of the Middle East, she found herself stationed right in the middle of Afghanistan. She was working as a floor nurse and completing checkups on recently injured soldiers. As she walked down the sterile, mostly quiet hallway there was a bearded, quite handsome man leaning against the wall.

"Can I help you with something sir?", she asked. Kelsey almost couldn't look at him and she started to blush a little. Jesus, Kelsey what is wrong with you she thought to herself. She wasn't accustomed to reacting this way as she had always been in control, especially since she worked alongside so many men throughout the years.

"You sure can ma'am, you can go back down that hallway and walk my way again because the closer you got the greener your eyes got and I'm pretty sure I just fell in love with you."

Kelsey put her clipboard over her face as it was turning red. "Sir, how did you get back here?'

"I walked right through those doors there". he said as he turned and pointed toward the way he'd come in. "See, the lady up front was mean and the line was taking too long to move so I figured I'd come back here and find someone who would help me.

And see how this turned out? Not just someone did, my future wife did!"

"C'mon now who around here put you up to this?" Kelsey asked.

"No one ma'am, I'm being honest. I have an appointment and everything." He couldn't take his eyes off her.

Kelsey looked up and they locked eyes for five seconds before she had to look away. She knew she was in trouble as the man reached his hand out to shake hers.

"Pretty lady, my name is Daxton Shaw, but my friends and family call me Dax."

CHAPTER FIVE

The Cessna Citation sat outside the private hangar as the sun began to set below the surface of the bay. Daxton slowly walked around the aircraft. He ran his hand down the edge of the wing and tapped on the aileron. He walked to the other side and pulled the cover off the pitot tube and pushed it back into his back pocket. He pulled some fuel from the wing and checked the clarity as he flung the fuel from his fuel tester. He stopped and looked out over the bay and the sunlit ripples dancing on the water. Daxton had looked at things in a different way after spending time in war-stricken places around the world. He was second-guessing not letting his daughter tag along on this trip, but he knew these guys were just a bit more than he wanted to expose her to. His thoughts were interrupted, and the silence was broken when he heard the loud laughs and hoots coming from inside the hangar. He shook his head and smiled thinking "Looks like the motley crew of 5 have arrived." He bounced up the stairs into the plane where he scooted into the left seat and started turning on the electronics one by one. The men started making their way into the plane.

"You guys just get the fuck in the plane, y'all can tell each other the bullshit lies on the way! God knows we've heard them all by now anyway!" he laughed as they climbed the stairs into the Cessna Citation.

JT, Daxton's life long best friend pushed his way past the pack of men and into the cockpit. He grabbed Daxton in a headlock and rubbed his head. "You miss me, dude? It's been a whole fuckin' minute, hasn't it?" Jesus, it's good to see you! I'm really looking forward to catching up brother."

Daxton pushed his way out of the headlock and pulled a punch into JT's kidney area. "Get the hell out of my cockpit, how long since you had a damn shower you stinky bastard?"

They laughed and bantered back and forth until Daxton's cousin Jonas stuck his head around the corner.

"My cousin the Jarhead!" Daxton smiled and stood up from his seat and the two of them embraced in a giant bear hug. "Jonas, man I am so glad you could make the trip with us. I didn't think Laura was going to let your ass out of the house with that new baby girl around."

Jonas pushed Daxton back to arm's length to look closely at him. "I'm driving her fucking nuts Dax, when she heard we were talking about taking this trip she said she'd sell one of her kidneys to fund my part." The two cousins laughed about the wives and Daxton's phone kept going off.

"Let me grab this guy, it's Sky." Daxton sat back in his seat and answered his phone. "Hey pumpkin, what's going on? We're about to take off but I wanted to make sure you're okay. That's why I was calling earlier."

"Yea, Daddy, I'm fine. I just wanted to tell you one more time that I was mad at you that I wasn't invited."

Daxton chuckled as he scanned the cockpit. "Look, pumpkin, I told you this wasn't a place for a young woman to be hanging around."

"I know, but I still wanted to make you feel bad and tell you that you owe me a trip!" Skyler teased.

"Deal, now go give your mother the phone, I love you very much," he replied. "I'll send you and your Mom some pictures as I get reception."

"Okay, I can't wait. Love you too and bring home some fish!"

She ran over and handed Kelsey the phone. Skyler was the spitting image of him and had his sense of adventure, travel, and experiences. "Hey Kels, we are about to head out. I wanted to tell you I love you very much and hope you guys enjoy your girl time. I will be ready to come home to you ladies after being with these knuckleheads all week. Kelsey chuckled. "Yea right, y'all will be partying down and having a blast being away from all the wives. Just promise me you will be safe and come home to us. How bout that?" "Deal," Daxton said. "Okay, baby I love you, and shoot me a text when you guys touchdown. Tell the boys I said hello."

"I will Kels, I love you too. Text you soon baby." Daxton hung up the phone and couldn't help but smile.

After everyone was seated Daxton pulled up the radar. He had been tracking a storm and was planning to go around just to the southeast of their destination. He looked at it for a few minutes before he convinced himself that the storm wouldn't be an issue. Daxton was very familiar with navigating storms by land, sea, or air. He let everyone settle into the cabin as he went through his preflight just like every other time he'd done it for the past twenty-five years of flying.

He got up from his seat and walked back into the main cabin. He placed his fingers to his lips and whistled to the rowdy crew. "Listen up you derelicts! First off, I'm so glad to see all your faces and glad you get to see me. Second, this flight won't leave the ground until each and every one of you has a cold drink in your hands."

The men reached into the coolers and started passing around beers. "And finally wear your seatbelts, sit back, relax, and get ready to catch more damn permit and bonefish than you can handle in a weekend.!" The group was cheering, high-fiving, and obviously excited for the trip ahead.

"Oh yeah, the boring shit now. The flight will be about an hour and ten minutes, and we'll be cruising about a buck fifty.

There are some storms around our destination airport so it may get a little bumpy." The men were buckling up as Daxton walked back to the cockpit.

He put on his headset and made a clear call to the tower. The airplane sprang to life, and he throttled up as he headed toward the taxiway. The men were talking and laughing, having a good time already in the back of the plane. As Daxton was cleared for takeoff he pointed the aircraft south on the runway. He held the brakes, and throttled up high until the propellers were trying to pull the aircraft down the runway. He let off the brakes and the plane quickly accelerated south. As he gained enough airspeed Daxton slowly pulled back on the yoke and the aircraft rose into the air. As he cleared the foliage, he had a clear picture in front of him. The ominous storms he was following on his radar were now in clear sight. The lightning struck and the black and blues of the storm were much darker than he would have expected. He shook it off and knew he was capable of flying around the storm and landing elsewhere if that scenario played out.

The jet engines of the Citation hummed as Daxton slowly gained altitude into the cloudy skies above. He scanned his cluster and glass panel instruments as he gained more speed and altitude. He had a genuine passion for flight and aviation.

Something about the precise planning, the mechanics, and just the pleasure of being one of the few who got to play in the skies were the things that drew him to it. He slowly banked the aircraft and dipped the left wing. He wanted to go ahead and start getting some distance between himself and the storm ahead. The radar was showing substantial lightning in the area along with some strong wind gusts in different directions. Typically, the island storms started to fizzle out a bit as the daytime heating let up. But this storm was different, it was growing, and it was growing fast.

As the darkness fell Daxton looked off toward the northeast. A huge cloud-to-cloud lightning show revealed one of the largest thunderheads he had ever seen. As dangerous as it was it was absolutely a gorgeous thing to witness. He checked his flight path again and where the destination runway was in relation to the storm. "Well, shit." he said as he looked closer at the radar. The storm was building faster than he could have imagined it would. As fast as the jet was, he wasn't going to push it and put any of them in jeopardy for a fishing trip.

It would set them back a day and that was worth peace of mind. He could put the aircraft down on another runway not much further to the west. It wasn't much of an airport, but it would have to do. Daxton pulled up the field base office information just to make sure he had the runway length to land the jet. He had landed there a couple of times years ago but in a twin prop that he could get to a stop quickly. The runway was

3,510 feet long and Daxton knew he really needed about 2,800 give or take. He knew he could really put the brakes on if he needed to but didn't want to put unnecessary stress on the Cessna. It was owned by a friend of his that just wanted Daxton to get her up in the air as it had sat in the hangar for a couple of months.

Daxton turned on the intercom as the party was rolling on in the cabin. "Attention ladies and gentlemen, more ladies than gentlemen back there." he joked. This is your captain speaking. Due to not wanting to unlife myself or anyone else aboard we will be taking a slight detour to the west. If you open your windows on the right side of the aircraft, you will notice the giant storms that I've changed my mind about flying through."

The men moved over and peered out the passenger side windows a few at a time. "Yea, imma say I'm with Dax on this one. That's one massive ass storm!" The men could feel the aircraft peeling off a little further to the west and returned to their seats. Jonas wasn't a huge fan of flying and grabbed a handle of whiskey out of this backpack.

He took a couple of swigs off the bottle and stuffed it back into his bag. "You alright, Jonas?" Jonas nodded and closed his eyes.

"We're all here for ya buddy!" JT yelled as the engines got a little louder.

Daxton radioed the tower to gain clearance to alter his course and land at the new destination. "AMB22 Tower, this is Cessna N710JT requesting runway clearance in approximately forty to fifty minutes. Would like to alter course to come see you guys tonight."

"Cessna N710JT, you are clear to make the trip over and land anytime. We have no traffic in the area at the Moment."

Daxton reset his course and radioed back, "Thanks, guys. That storm off to the east looks like a plane eater and I have some real pansies aboard." The guy in the tower laughed and wished him safe travels for the next forty minutes of the flight.

The storm continued to build, and the lightning was spectacular as it lit up the sky. Daxton and his passengers burned thorough the night sky at about three hundred miles per hour toward their new destination for the night.

Daxton continued on his heading toward their new destination. He watched out of the right-seat window as the storm continued to grow. He knew he had made the right call dodging the weather and re-routing their course. JT entered the cockpit and jumped into the right seat. He was obviously a few drinks in and probably had a few before he even got onboard the plane. "My brother, it's so good to see you dude. We never get to see each other or hang out anymore. You had to go and move to paradise and leave us old saps behind." JT took a swig from his double IPA bottle. "I miss the crazy times we had and now look at us, flying a private jet through some storms down in the island chain headin' to catch some bones and permit. Thanks for everything man, you did so much for me and the family when I needed it. I just want you to know that."

Daxton was half-assed listening as he was checking his instruments. "You know I would do anything for you and the fam brother. Don't sweat it." Daxton answered.

JT started to buckle up the right seat, but Daxton reached over and unbuckled it. "Not tonight JT. This one is on me up here tonight bud."

"Aww. C'mon man, how many times have I sat right seat when you hit the deck?"

Daxton thought about it. JT was right, but Daxton wanted him in the back tonight, he wanted him to enjoy his time and just relax. "Probably a thousand. But not for this one, go get the guys riled up back there, tell them you had to wake me up or I was drinking alone up here. Make up some bullshit, you're good at it!" Daxton laughed.

JT winked at Daxton and tilted the rest of his beer up. "Well, you know I can at least handle that!" JT got up and kissed Daxton on the head. "Put us down safe brother, drinks on me when we land."

Daxton couldn't help but smile but it was time to get the plane on the ground. He called into the tower one more time as he started ascending from the dark skies over the moonlit waters.

Daxton could hear JT telling a story and laughing his ass off as he adjusted his headset. About the time he got them back on and comfortable the tower came over the radio. "Cessna N710JT This is AMB22 Tower. Do you copy?"

Daxton replied, "AMB22 Tower, copy here."

"Roger that, it looks like we have a bit of a situation here.

The storm, as you can see, is throwing off some random lightning strikes. Looks like one of the strikes hit close and knocked out the main power. The generators are up and running but the runway is only partially lit now, do you copy?"

"Copy that tower, all I need is a glimmer of a runway outline and I can get her down," Daxton replied.

"Copy Cessna N710JT, we will try to get them lit up as soon as possible. If you need to request a flyby, feel free." The tower responded,

"Thank you tower, we are about ten minutes out to have visual and I will confirm at that time." Daxton looked at all the instruments again before turning his head to the left. He was hoping the lightning would be sufficient, but he had landed aircraft in the jungles with small fires as lighting, he knew his capabilities. He came over the intercom. "Time to buckle up guys. And tighten them' up just a little extra. This may be a little bumpier than usual due to some of the winds in the area." He could see them in the cabin through the camera in the cockpit.

His passengers were all in their seats and in the process of buckling up. "See all you scallywags on the ground shortly and thanks for flying with us at Crashem and Burnem Airlines. All of them laughed and pulled open their windows. Daxton reached over and hit the record button on his GoPro that was attached to the dash. He liked to capture the Moments and make videos of his travels alone and with his family.

He lined up about five miles away and started searching for the light on the runway. As he neared the runway, he looked at his glass and knew it would be coming into view. He squinted as he passed the lower clouds looking for the landing strip lights. "They weren't kidding, were they? Okay, Dax let's get her in nice and safely as always." he thought. "AMB22 Tower, this is Cessna N710JT coming in on final approach."

As Daxton approached the runway, he dropped his airspeed to around 130 knots and dropped the ailerons. It was definitely much darker than he anticipated, and he could barely make out the lights in front of him. The left side was almost completely invisible, but he could see it off and on. He dropped to 700', 500' 300', and then 100'. He could make out the runway a little easier and see that his alignment was just about spot on. He felt a little calmer knowing he was lined up. He dropped lower and lower and as he began to flair the aircraft nose up for landing his eyes went wide and his heartbeat increased. "What the………. HOLD O…" Things instantly went into slow motion for Daxton, and he braced for impact.

Before he could get out the blood-curdling scream the aircraft's left wing and a partial section of the fuselage collided with the aircraft tug that sat on the runway. The left-wing exploded into pieces and was completely severed. The fuselage started ripping to pieces following the complete destruction of the wing. It was utter chaos as the men were screaming and the aircraft quickly started coming apart. The landing gear was ripped from the front of the aircraft, and it slid across the asphalt throwing a hundred-foot spray of sparks as the steel and aluminum dug into the runway. The ungodly sounds of the twisting steel and wreckage pierced everyone's ears. The plane started to slide sideways and off the runway. It bounced violently through a small ditch and from the bounce Daxton's head was smashed against the side window. His vision went black, and he instantly went limp.

As the aircraft slid quickly across the grass the left side came apart and two of the men were killed instantly being rolled over by the mangled jagged steel sections of the fuselage. JT and Daxton's cousin Jonas were both knocked unconscious from the impact and dangled like rag dolls from their seatbelts. What was left of the Cessna slid into a group of palm trees and was then severed into two more sections that went rolling and twisting through the tropical foliage. Pieces flew from the plane that was now nothing more than twisted metal. The pieces slowly came to a stop and settled down into the mud.

JT was the first to come to, then Daxton shortly after. All they could hear were sirens going off from the plane, pieces of metal still cracking and hissing, and trees breaking and snapping. They could both smell the melting plastic and jet fuel.

Daxton reached up as he could feel the blood gushing from a massive gash on his head, and he stuck his finger into the wound. His adrenaline was so high he felt no pain. "Dammit! He knew it was a bad gaping wound. He unclipped his seatbelt and fell to the ground as sparks from the electronics rained down upon him. He screamed loudly in agony as his left arm was shattered and a piece of metal pierced through his forearm. "Ahhhh, Jesus, Hey! Anybody???" He slowly pulled himself up with his other arm. "Helloooo……Anyone out there?" Helloooo! He screamed so loudly his voice cracked in agony. He pulled himself along the ground toward the other pieces of the plane.

JT could hear Daxton screaming in the distance and his ears rang almost to the point of being deaf from it. Daxton's voice was muffled but he could hear it. He looked over and could see Daxton's cousin dangling upside down as blood ran down his arms and dripped off his fingertips.

"Jonas!!" JT yelled at Daxton's cousin. He kept yelling and could hear Daxton's voice getting closer and closer.

"Dax!! Daaaxxx! We're here, we're over here!" JT looked down at this seatbelt and went to pull the release latch. His right pinky finger was only attached by a small piece of skin.

He pulled the latch open with his left hand and the belt came loose. He rolled out of the mangled section and down onto the ground. Daxton got to JT and put his arms around his friend. "Are you okay? Have you seen the others?"

JT mumbled that he was okay as blood poured from his mouth. "We've got to get your cousin down Dax. He's in bad shape dude but I think he's alive. I don't know about the others."

Daxton limped toward Jonas and started screaming.

"Jonas, wake up! Wake up!" He could smell and see the AV gas seeping into the ground, and he knew he had to get Jonas down now. JT was screaming at Jonas and limping toward Daxton.

Daxton was trying to climb up the side to reach Jonas' seatbelt. 'I can get it JT! I almost got it! "He fell and slid down the side of the metal wall. A blood smear from his side left a trail on the metal. The two men yelled at the top of their lungs and Daxton thought he saw Jonas's arm move.

"He's waking up JT, keep yelling!" Daxton tried but was helpless and too far away to unlatch Jonas's seatbelt.

They kept yelling but received no response from Jonas.

As they yelled the runway and foliage looked like a war zone. There were fires and pieces of jagged metal strewn out for a thousand yards. As they continued to yell a small fire broke out near the aircraft that caught JT's eye.

"Fuck Daxton run! Run now! Fire!" Daxton wasn't moving so JT grabbed him and turned him around and pushed him. "God dammit go Daxton!! It's going to blow!"

JT and Daxton only made it about thirty feet away before the small flame made its way along the leading edge of the mangled wing. The flame slowly went into the fuel tank and the last remaining piece of the aircraft erupted into a massive explosion. The fireball rose high into the air as the explosion ripped through the trees sending remnants of the aircraft pieces through the forest like projectiles. The two of them were violently blown off their feet and completely knocked unconscious before they even hit the ground.

Large raindrops fell from the dark clouds of the island skies. The rain hissed as it made contact with the melting pieces of the aircraft. Black smoke bellowed into the sky and over the palm trees and two men lay in shambles in the mud as the rain and wind picked up from the approaching storm.

CHAPTER SIX

The rain poured on the steel roof as Daxton lay in his bed watching the ceiling fan slowly turn. For the last two years every time he closed his eyes at night, he could hear the explosions, the screams and almost smelled the jet fuel. As he reached over and grabbed his half-empty whisky bottle, lightning cracked and lit up his room. He quickly glanced at a photo of himself and Skyler on the summit of Mount Baldy. He clenched his eyes tightly and tilted the whisky bottle back one more time for the night. He picked up the pill container from his side table, took out a pill, and swallowed it washing it down with one more slug from the bottle. After a few minutes, he fell back onto his pillow and slowly fell into a numbing daze. His mind settled down for a Moment and the noise of the ceiling fan turned into the sounds inside of the hospital. The nurses all came into the room. "It's about time you meet your beautiful new daughter Mr. Shaw!" Daxton looked at Kelsey with pure excitement, he kissed her on the forehead and slid his chair back while still embracing her hand.

Shortly after the nurses and doctor delivered Skyler, he heard her cries for the first time. Daxton was in tears as the nurse handed Skyler up to Kelsey. The three of them snuggled in and Daxton and Kelsey cried together as a family for the first time. A quick vision of Kelsey in her wedding dress flashed through his mind. He could see how beautiful she was, like an angel standing under the small rock bridge just waiting to say yes to him and start their life adventure together.

He had visions of Skyler growing up, singing, swimming, school, and climbing with him played out in his mind like a movie reel.

His brother-in-law Jonas walked out from a shadowy hallway and smiled. He reached out his hand to shake and Daxton went in for a hug. The two of them said nothing in the dream but Daxton could feel his brother and friend yet again.

Daxton could see Skyler throwing her cap into the air at her graduation and feel Kelsey's lips make contact with his cheek. He could feel the breeze of the air on the lake as he listened to the laughs from his wife and daughter as the boat peeled through the water.

As the night went on some of Daxton's greatest memories flooded into his dreams. There were no night sweats, no tossing and turning, no waking up for another swig of his whiskey. Daxton was typically an earlier riser but on that morning the sun and sound of the chickens woke him up. The beam of sunshine through the window slowly crept up the sheets, gleemed off of his compass necklace then into his face. He wiped his eyes and was perplexed that he had actually slept in so late. He looked over at this side table at the whisky bottle. "Usually there's none left in that." He thought to himself. His soul felt clean, he felt rested and for once in a very long time, clear-headed.

He jumped out of bed and grabbed the whisky bottle and a towel as he headed for the shower. He looked at the bottle, turned it upside down in the sink, and watched the amber liquid go down the drain. He threw the bottle into the trash can, flung his towel over the shower door, and jumped into the shower.

As he ran his hands through his hair the memories of his dreams slowly began to creep back in. He smiled and started singing "Sweet Caroline" while he wrapped up in the shower.

They had taught Skyler how to sing that song with them when she could just barely talk. They had probably sung it a thousand times on their guided dive and fishing trips. He finished his shower, checked his phone, and quickly got dressed for the day.

He made his way out the door and down the stairs where one of the locals was cooking breakfast on an open flame, over a steel drum. "Heya there, Mr. Dax! You want breakfast and a beer this morning sir?" Workday huh?"

Daxton smiled and approached his cooking buddy. He grabbed him and hugged him tightly. "Not today, Carlo, not today but I will tell you that my door is open and there is a case or more in the fridge. Why don't you have a beer on me for a change this morning? You know what Carlo, have them all!"

Carlo looked dumbfounded but wasn't going to turn down that offer. "You got it, boss, just put me in bed if I'm still out here when you get back."

The two of them laughed as Daxton jumped onto his 1979 Honda CBX motorcycle to go get Skyler and head to the marina.

Daxton took a deep breath of the cooler humid air, He put his shades on, fired up his motorcycle, and headed down the dirt path into town with a much lighter feeling and a happier heart.

CHAPTER SEVEN

Skyler Shaw was twenty years old when she left for Florida Southwestern. She never really applied herself to school but always seemed to make the grade, it came to easy for her which in turn made her bored as well very easily. At a young age, she spent a lot of time with her father traveling with him on his short flights and dive charters. It was almost impossible for Daxton to walk out the door with his flight bag or God forbid any type of dive gear. Skyler would run and grab her coral-colored "adventure" backpack which Daxton had made her and straight for the door she would head. At the time the backpack almost dragged the ground as it was just as big as she was. Most of the time her Mom would have no issue with it as she knew that Daxton would never let anything happen to his princess. They had talked about trying for another one in hopes of maybe getting their son, but as Skyler grew up, they realized they had the best of both worlds. Skyler stood about 5'6" with a firm build. She played volleyball and swam all through high school and it's about the only things that kept her there at school. She was a very active young woman and kept her athletic physique after high school. Skyler wore her hair short and was a natural dirty blonde. Her dad always joked that her mom couldn't wear her hair short because it would expose her horns.

Skyler got her SCUBA cert at the age of sixteen after she fell in love with being underwater. Daxton would sit her in a lawn chair at the bottom of the pool and let her breathe off his SCUBA rig for almost an hour at times. She probably had more bottom time by age ten than most divers do in years of diving. Skyler was trained in search and rescue, night diving, nitrox, and was an assistant dive instructor by the time she was eighteen years old. It's what she wanted to do in life, dive, travel, instruct, and see the world. Although both Daxton and Kelsey shared her sense of adventure, they wanted more for her than just to be a dive bum. She worked as a dive instructor and guide for so many of the charters that Daxton ran. People could not help but fall in love with her, she had a gorgeous smile and laugh and such an insatiable passion for the water and teaching. Reluctantly Skyler agreed to go to school to at least get some kind of degree. She selected history just to learn more about the past and geography of the world. She worked at the dive shop near the lake while going to school to fuel her passion and stay involved and connected in the dive world.

The phone rang in front of the dive shop. "Cameron, can you grab that for me? I've got my hands full!" Skyler yelled through the swinging doors from the back as she struggled to clip the pieces of the rebreather rig back together. The phone rang 4 or 5 more times as surf music played over the store speakers. "Cameron can you please just get the phone? Jesus dude!"

Cameron stumbled out of the side door and slowly headed for the ringing phone. "Tony's Dive Hut, how can I help you? He answered in slow surfer slang. "Ohhhh, Hey Mrs. Shaw, yea she's in the back doing something I guess, I will go get her for you." Cameron covered the speaker on the phone with his hand. "SKYLER, it's your Mom on the phone! She needs to talk to you."

Skyler almost had the retainer clip back in place as Cameron swung the doors open. "Hey dude your Mom...." The retainer clip flew out of the pliers and buzzed past Cameron's head. "You trying to kill me or what? I said your Mom is on the phone." Skyler glazed at Cameron. "I heard you! I've been trying to get that damn clip in for an hour!" She ran by Cameron busted through the double doors and headed for the phone. "Hey Mom, I know I need to be back early tonight before you say anything."

"Why hello to you too missy, Its fine baby. I just wanted to call to tell you to take a few days off of work. We have a little trip planned and I know you won't want to miss this one."

"I really cant Mom, we have training coming up in a few days and we are already shorthanded, I'm just not sure we can...." Kelsey interrupted Skyler. "We are going to go see your Dad."

"Dad? But why? Why are we going to see him? Is he okay Mom?" Skyler could feel the blood rush into her face as she began to panic. "There is no need to worry Skyler, your father is just fine, I mean other than him just being himself.

I will completely explain when you get here. Liam actually has some business where your Dad is and I think he wants your Dad to take him and some business partners marlin fishing as well. We are taking Liam's plane and plan on leaving sometime tomorrow." Skyler hated Liam but she knew that if they were going to see her father she was not going to miss the opportunity.

She told her mother she was leaving to go ahead and come home to pack.

Skyler yelled at Cameron. "Cameron, can you hold it down for a few days? We don't have any rentals coming or going so it should be pretty quiet. I have a chance to go see my Dad down in Mexico and I am not missing out." "I got you Bruh, be safe, and don't worry about it here. Go see your Dad and have a good time"

Skyler grabbed her tattered coral-colored backpack from the back of the chair and slung it over her shoulder as she headed out the front of the dive shop. Her mind was going in 1000 directions and thoughts of her father flooded into her head.

CHAPTER EIGHT

The iridescent flashes of blue welding light penetrated through the dense jungle canopy. The makeshift building facility was in full swing working on the current vessel build that had been recently paid for by a new customer involved in the high-profile smuggling business.

A black helicopter slowly sank below the canopy line and settled into the damp terrafirma. The helicopter engine shut down and as the blades began to slow the passenger door slid open. A slender dark-haired man and three other men climbed out and headed toward the entrance to the facility.

The slender man pulled a cigarette from his pocket, placed it between his lips, and lit the end. He took a deep drag and surveyed the area. "What a giant shithole, I expected a little more bang for my buck!" he said arrogantly. He picked up his expensive leather shoe from the mud and looked at the mess. "Shall we see how they are progressing with our investment gentlemen?"

The four men walked up to the door that was flanked by two armed guards. As they stepped closer to the entrance, the guards raised their weapons in warning. "Easy gentlemen, you see most of my investments at the moment are tied up behind that door and we will be going in to check the progress regardless of who tells you otherwise."

One of the guards reached down to grab his radio. As he touched his radio one of the visitors slung the MP5 he was carrying into his face. The guard let his M16 slide to his side and put his hands in the air.

"Tell them Liam is here to pay a little checkup visit."

The guard slowly reached down to retrieve his radio and spoke to someone inside the building. There was a brief discussion and the guard reached over to the massive sliding door and cracked it enough for the four men to enter.

The sleek black submarine was sitting in a cradle and there were over fifteen men working in the area. Wires were strung across the floor and boxes of electronics were lying next to the sub.

"Please, don't stop working on my account now guys, we need this beautiful piece of art done yesterday!" Liam shouted while he smoked his cigarette. "Now, who is in charge and speaks some fucking English around here?" The men looked at each other and didn't say anything. Liam asked again, "Who the fuck is in charge of this operation?" He flicked his cigarette onto the sub and grabbed one of the men by his sleeve.

"I run this operation, and you can get your cigarette off my build, or you and your cronies can find your way out of my shop!" Mateo said as he walked out of the side door. He wiped his hands on a towel. "Can I help you with something? No one told me we were going to have visitors this evening, especially a loudmouth asshole!"

I just figured the chopper was a visit from the boss and now I have some strangers walking into my facility flicking fucking cigarettes on a tightly sealed vessel worth well over a million bucks."

At this point, Liam walked over to Mateo scowling. "I pay your salary; I own this million-dollar submarine and I can ask any question I want."

Mateo walked up to him and looked down at this stature. "You don't sign a fucking thing around here. I didn't get word that I needed to give you a tour. You guys sign my check, ok, so for that, I will show you around. That's the only reason! Now, get your cigarette off MY project and we will give you the grand tour. But for that, I will need to see your credentials."

Liam was miffed but he complied knowing it was in his best interest to stay on Mateo's better side.

"We aren't ready for site visits just yet, but we will show you what we have up to date."

Liam walked around looking at the flat black slender vessel. It was approximately seventy feet in length and only eight feet wide. Liam peered down into the open hull.

"This is much smaller than I thought it was going to be, I specifically said that we needed plenty of payload area and this is not that," Liam grumbled.

Mateo faced Liam. "I designed this vessel from tip to tip. I was given specific criteria when it came to payload size and weight. I don't care and I didn't ask what the payload will be, Mateo lied, just cubic feet and weight of material to be moved. That's what I was given and that's what will fit into this submarine.

Liam glared at Mateo and the two of them stared each other down. Then Liam looked back and scanned the sub while he started walking down the pier that flanked the vessel. "Why is it so thin in width?"

Mateo pulled a folded-up drawing from his back pocket and held it up. "I designed it to be sleek, fast, and not cause much of an outline signature. She can also drop deeper and quicker with the sharp keel and narrow hull. I can get her down twenty to thirty feet deep in seconds."

Liam nodded and liked what he was hearing. "Tell me about what makes this one so much more expensive than the others I put bids on to build to specifications. I know I was told by your employer, but I want to hear it from the man who designed it and is sweating it out watching it come together."

Mateo waved Liam to follow him into the small makeshift office and Liam signaled for the others to stay behind. He followed Mateo inside, and Mateo closed and locked the door behind them. Mateo flipped on the large overhead lights. Large drawings and schematics lined the four walls of the room. White boards were everywhere with equations and designs in different colors.

"This is not your normal cocaine running sub thrown together by the cheapest bid or by forcing the build at gunpoint. This is a one-of-a-kind engineered, procured, and constructed underwater transport vessel. I spent thousands of hours just in the design phase, I have called on specialists from the propeller design, ballast displacements, electronics, radar, and remote systems. This is one of a kind and will also be a vessel that you can reuse, resell, or rent out." Mateo explained.

Liam peered around the room and looked at all the blueprints as he shook his head. "I am feeling much better about this and the fact that you tell me we can reuse and rent, that gets my thoughts going and I feel better about the purchase price."

Liam walked around the small room and peered closer at the drawings. "I see no place for the captain, where will he sit, and do you have that man selected?"

Mateo grabbed a plastic box off the shelf and placed it on the table. He flipped the latches of the box and pulled out its contents. The piece was just a bit larger than a basketball and was sitting on a square base. Liam leaned in and could see his reflection in the black mirrored globe.

"This is the captain. Meet ROME, Remote Operated Marine Equipment. He doesn't panic, he doesn't have anxiety, get sick, turn around, rat you out, or ask for any extra money."

Liam's eyes lit up. "Genius! But can anyone else take over? Hack into the system and steal the sub?"

Mateo replied, "No, absolutely not! It's been deemed unhackable and we had the best equipment and the best system in the world that can't be touched."

Liam shook his head in disbelief. "And what if it gets confiscated? Then what? They see what technology we can utilize now in this industry?"

"We have parameters built in for that as well. The ballast system will pull in fifty gallons per second to drop the sub at a quick rate. There is a cooling system on the top side of the hull and in the engine compartment that will throw off the heat signature that the sub will emit. Once the sub is deep enough and shuts down it can maintain the depth as long as the threat remains nearby. If all hell breaks loose and there are no other options, there is a five-step process to implode the vessel into pieces that could not be traced."

Liam looked confused. "You said implode, so basically, you'd be blowing up MY million-dollar plus submarine if you feel a threat. Who gets to make that decision?"

Mateo walked over to the table and started putting the ROME unit back into its case. "I'm just building this thing, that's something out of my pay grade that you will have to take up with the boss."

Liam gleamed at Mateo. "And that will be a conversation that we will have before she departs. I can assure you of that."

Mateo walked toward the door and motioned Liam out as he shut down the lights, closed the door placed the lock back on the hasp, and closed it tightly. "We really need to get back to work on this. I was told it needed to be completed and have two test runs under her belt in the next four weeks. We have a long way to go."

Liam took another look around at the sub and motioned for his men to head toward the exit. "We will be on our way then, thank you for the tour and please tell your boss I will be in contact about this whole imploding situation,"

Mateo was quiet as the men exited the building and he slid the door closed behind them. He walked back over to his area and picked up his cell phone. The helicopter could be heard firing up in the background as he made his report. "Hey boss, yeah, they are gone. Just wanted to let you know to expect a call from our surprise visitor." Mateo could hear the helicopter lift off and knew the canopy of the jungle was blowing in all directions as the lights lit up the sky. The visitor was gone, and it was time to get back to work.

CHAPTER NINE

Mateo's moped headlight bounced up and down on the brick road as he made it into the small island town. The town was bustling with people, some walking and others riding their mopeds and motorcycles through town. He pulled into the small corner cantina and dropped the kickstand on the moped to the ground. There was a storm off In the distance and he looked at the lightning in the sky.

"Mateo! Where have you been my friend? We thought the jungle ate you up!" Mateo smiled as the owner reached around him and escorted him into the cantina. Mateo found his empty seat at the weathered bar and pulled his chair in close. He had already thought about what he would tell anyone who might ask what he had been working on. "You are right Andreas; the jungle ate me. And I'll have a double of Ron Viejo."

Andreas reached to the top shelf and grabbed a bottle of Ron. "Well, the jungle must pay you well my friend." He poured the double in a dirty low-ball glass and slid it over to Mateo.

Mateo put the glass to his lips and downed about half the liquid and dropped it back onto the bar. "I got a call from an American-based company; they are installing some weather stations throughout the jungle they would like to monitor from the states. Something about how the canopy being reduced drops humidity and kills some little frogs. I don't care. I just knew it paid well."

Andreas refilled the half-full glass to the top. "Sounds boring as hell Mateo. I was thinking it would be cocaine, subs, or something more interesting than that." He winked at Mateo as he placed the bottle back on the shelf.

Mateo took a deep breath. He could feel his face getting flushed and he knew that Andreas was way too close to the truth to have just thrown that notion out. Mateo was an educated man, he was in tune with all the latest technology. He spent hours studying and learning technology and served in the National Army of Columbia. With all that background he was not a good poker player and an even worse liar. He pulled a few more sips of his drink as his phone vibrated on the bar top, He looked down and his phone notification. "We start at 5:00 am tomorrow. The schedule has been changed." Mateo's trip would be much shorter than he expected. He didn't have the courage to go home as his wife knew what he was doing and had shunned him for taking the project. He put his elbows on the bar and dropped his head into his hands. About the time he collected his thoughts, a well-built man sat next to him on a barstool. He wore a white tank top, and a pair of shorts and had his black hair slicked back. His 5 o'clock shadow was obviously a few days old. He looked toward Andreas, "Good evening my good man. Can I get a vodka martini? Ohh, you know what. Hold that thought. Let's just do a Russian vodka on ice. I hear they make some exceptional vodka among other things."

Andreas looked over at the new patron and pulled some Svedka off the shelf telling him, "This is what we have tonight."

The patron threw up his hands and said, "That's what I'll have then." He nudged Mateo on the shoulder. "Nice place huh? Do you come here often?"

Mateo slowly looked over at the man. "For about twenty years. And yes, it is a nice place. Always has been." The man shook his head as Andreas pushed his glass of vodka over.

He took a drink and said, "So local huh?"

Mateo shook his head yes and took a drink. "I don't want to be rude, but I'm exhausted, and I have to be at work at 5. I'm not much for small talk right now" The man picked up his vodka and slowly poured the rest of the drink into his mouth. He swished it around and swallowed the contents. "I completely understand you are on a tight schedule for project Submarine. It's a big undertaking and just the idea of the payload it's going to carry. My God" The man got louder. Mateo looked around the cantina and back at the man. "I don't know what you're talking about!" Mateo said loudly.

The stranger laughed briefly while he spun his finger in the air at Andreas for another round. "The fuck you don't Mateo Cruz. The strangers demeanor changed like the flip of a switch. "Well, your wife said much different when we spoke to her."

Mateo jumped off his stool and leaped after the man. "Who are you, you asshole, you don't know my wife!"

Andreas came around the bar and grabbed Mateo and pulled him off the man. The man stood up and took his seat back at the bar while Mateo wrestled Andreas back as he slowly let go and calmed down. Meanwhile, the man pulled a card out of his front pocket and handed it to Mateo. He looked directly into his eyes, "I am afraid I am already familiar with your whole family Mr. Cruz. Every. Single. One of them. Here is my contact information and I suggest you call me on a pay phone in the next three days to arrange a formal meeting. If you don't there will be dire consequences. If you do and we come to terms you and your family will never have to worry about money again."

The life drained out of Mateo, and he knew that the guy was serious. He could feel this was no bluff. The man took the card out of Mateo's hand and placed it in his front pocket.

"Wouldn't want you to lose this he said as he patted Mateo's shoulder. So, now I'm going to walk out of here, you aren't going to call anyone or talk to anyone about this. You will call me in the next three days, and I will know if you alert anyone. I'm looking forward to our visit soon, Mr. Cruz."

CHAPTER TEN

Daxton pulled the speed back and threw in some ailerons as he lined up the nose of the Cessna 182 toward the runway. His Bluetooth speaker was blaring some Bob Marley and he couldn't help smiling knowing he was about to see his daughter. The sun danced on the waters off in the distance and there wasn't a cloud in the sky. He didn't drink the day or night before. His head was clear, and he felt alive, all his senses were working, with the exception of being a bit shaky. He could see the black SUV sitting by the hangar and a few people standing around. He tipped the left wing twice as he always did when Skyler was watching him come in for a landing. His wheels hit the asphalt runway and he bailed off to the tarmac toward the hangars. As he pulled closer, he could see Skyler waving her hand up with a huge smile on her face. Daxton stopped the small aircraft and shut everything down. He threw the headset into the right seat and jumped out of the plane. Daxton had on a long-sleeved fishing shirt, board shorts, and flip-flops. Skyler ran toward the plane and when she reached him she gave him the biggest hug Daxton had ever gotten. "Sky, Jesus' girl, you're a full grown-ass woman! I have missed you so much!"

Skyler pushed him back after their hug saying, "Well, Daddy? Where is it?"

Daxton smiled and walked back to the plane as Skyler followed. "Not just one this time Sky, been a few places since I last came up to see you." He pulled out five small glass containers filled with sand. All were labeled with longitude and latitude. "I missed a couple, but I was just trying to leave a few for you to get yourself." She smiled and hugged Daxton around the neck again.

Daxton would always pick up sand for Skyler from all the places he had been from the time she was very young. It didn't matter whether is was an exotic place or not, he always got her a piece of earth from his destinations. Skyler had the jars lined on the shelves in her room. She also had a map that she would poke pins into that indicated the coordinates that he put on the jars.

"Well, 'Imma let it slide this time Daddy. But there's a lot of other shit I'm not going to let slide."

"Skyler! Mouth girl!" Daxton said through his smile.

She smirked at him and held back what she really wanted to say. Now was not the time to hash out the last two and a half years.

Daxton could see Kelsey and Liam standing by the hangar looking in their direction. "He's looking all hot and sassy these days, isn't he? Come help me get this little bird in the hangar and then we'll go say hello." Skyler went over to the other side of the fuselage and together they pushed the plane toward the hangar. "Dad, please play nice. Mom's having a rough time these days."

"Is she? Why? Is he putting his hands on her?" Daxton questioned.

"No Dad, calm down, she's just been in a weird place, that's all. Can we all be adults here? They need you to help and want to help you." Skyler told him.

"Don't think I really asked for it Sky, but for you absolutely, I will play adult."

Kelsey and Liam joined them in the hangar and Daxton looked at Liam. "Dude, you got more in that suit than I do in this fine piece of flight machinery. Can you throw me those wheelchocks bud?" Liam looked to Kelsey, and she gave him a nod to help so he awkwardly ran over and fumbled with the wheel chock that hung from the ropes. He put them in front of the tire. "Both sides of the tire Lyle. I meant Liam." Daxton told him. Liam pushed the chocks under both sides of the tire and stood looking for affirmation.

"You sure know your way around a hangar, maybe you can just come down here and work for me!" Daxton walked over to Liam. Liam held out his hand for a handshake and Daxton gave him a big hug instead. "Enough with the handshake, we are practically family bud!"

Skyler looked at her Mom and just shook her head. Daxton had a way of breaking the ice in a different way than most would. Liam looked at Kelsey and she just shrugged her shoulders.

Then Daxton walked over to Kelsey. "How was the private jet ride down? Hope he had enough Cabernet on board to calm those old nerves of yours down." Kelsey looked deeply into Daxton's eyes, and they locked in for a few seconds. Daxton looked away but she could feel his sadness and knew that he was all smoke and mirrors for this meeting. He was hurting. He was fighting to be the man that he used to be. It could have been for her, but she knew it was for Skyler.

Daxton clapped his hands, "Speaking of Cab, I know a little place up the road where we can catch up, grab a drink, and visit about why we're all here together. How's that sound?"

No one disagreed with him, so Liam and Skyler joined him and Kelsey. Daxton pulled his phone out of his pocket. "I know a one-armed cab driver that can get us over there, rides on me. Don't mind the smell or the weird convo but she's the best around here."

Liam glanced at Kelsey. "It's okay Daxton, we have a vehicle here waiting but thank you for the offer and such gracious hospitality."

Daxton put his phone back in his pocket and hugged Skyler. "Suit yourself, no one ever tells stories about riding in a 2024 Suburban by a guy dressed up in some Versace getup."

Liam motioned for them to all head to the SUV and as the drivers opened the doors to let them in Daxton couldn't help himself and said, "I feel like Tom Cruise or something with all this grand treatment. He looked at Skyler and winked as he got into the SUV.

After they were settled in the vehicle Liam said to Daxton, "Thank you for coming Daxton. I really appreciate you considering to help us with this matter. I want to be honest; you weren't my first option. But you are the best, and I hear you could use a break.

Daxton pulled the champagne from the small side cooler and popped the cork. He took a slug from the bottle and pushed it back into the ice. "I am not the best and I haven't considered anything at this point. I am here because my daughter asked me to be. I don't need a break. I don't need your money or you down here making a mess of these islands. I know your type; I know what you're about. I despise men like you who ship weapons all over the world, so guys like me get hit with bullets you send and don't come back to their families." Daxton took a deep breath. "Okay, we got that out of the way. Let's go grab that drink. "Driver, take us over to the Salty Shrimp."

The all-terrain tires crunched the small pebbles on the caleche road as the SUV headed out of the airport gates toward town.

CHAPTER ELEVEN

The Black SUV pulled into the busy dirt parking lot. "Well, it looks like we made it, you guys are going to love this place! Remember that old place we used to go to Sky when you were just a little bit?"

"The Pier?" Skyler instantly responded.

"That's the one Sky. Daxton slung open the door as the driver walked around to open Liam's door. Liam looked like a fish out of water. "I'm sure it's going to be great just judging by its character" Liam commented snidely as he helped Kelsey exit the vehicle.

Daxton slid up next to Skyler and put his arm around her shoulder as they walked toward the restaurant door. "I can't wait to hear about your new adventures. I'm sure you'll have some stories to tell me. Oh yeah, and about school too." Skyler pushed him in a playful way. Daxton held the door for everyone and as Liam neared the door with Kelsey Daxton caught Liam. "Heads up Liam, so you're just going to let your driver sit in there and not come eat with us? Who are you? Some kind of animal? That man takes care of you and MY family. He needs to come break bread with us."

Liam looked at Kelsey and she shook her head in approval.

"Okay then, I'm going to go get him." Daxton said.

As Liam, Kelsey, and Skyler disappeared into the restaurant Daxton ran out to the SUV. He knocked on the dark tinted windows and the man rolled it down. Daxton leaned in as the window rolled down. "Hey bud, you hungry?" The man looked at Daxton with a weird gaze. "No, I'm fine and don't need anything." Daxton shook his head and said, "Bullshit, I know you've been traveling for six hours just since I've been with you. You weigh about a solid two-fifty and obviously, you are missing your protein intake for the day to keep those big guys fed." Daxton squeezed the big man's arm. The driver glared at him and pushed Daxton's hand off telling him "I'm fucking starving, and I can spot a devil dog a mile away. You sure it's okay with the boss?"

"Screw your boss, he's a douche and you're going to have dinner with a comrade this evening. "What's your name, big fella?" Daxton reached his hand into the window. The big man reluctantly grabbed Daxtons hand and shook it. "Scott." He said in a big deep voice. "Good deal Scott, I'm Daxton Shaw, now let your swelled-up ass out of the truck and come and eat." Liam's driver reluctantly got out of the SUV and followed Daxton. "Thatta boy! Now let's go grab some dinner!"

They made their way to the reservation counter where Liam stood. Daxton pushed his way through the group to the counter. A younger girl smiled and walked around the counter to give Daxton a hug. "Hey, Dax! Where have you been lately? Is this your family?" Daxton turned and pointed everyone out in the group telling her, "That's it, all of us just one big happy fam dam!"

The hostess went to Skyler and introduced herself. "Nine out of ten stories your Dad tells involve you, you are so lucky to have a Dad like that," she told Skyler.

Skyler looked at her Dad and smiled. "Yeah, he's pretty great. I just miss him. Before she got into her feelings she brushed it off.

Daxton caught sight of Kalea who was working behind the bar. Daxton smirked and waved her to come over to the group. Kalea smiled walked around the bar and headed in their direction. About that time Kelsey looked up and could see the way Kalea was looking at Daxton. She was gorgeous, tan, and vuloptious and didn't mind wearing an outfit that was made for the beach. Kelsey shook her head knowing Daxton's charm had obviously worked on this beautiful exotic woman approaching them. She came over to Daxton, wrapped her arms around his neck, and kissed him on the lips. "Well Dax, you need to introduce me to your family. I have been dying to meet you all. As confident as Daxton was he actually started to blush and turn a little red. "Well, Kalea this is my daughter Skyler." Before Daxton could say more Kalea rushed over and gave Skyler a giant hug. Skyler looked back at Daxton with a panic in her eyes. "I knew the second I saw you come in you were Skyler, I have heard so much about you and you are so beautiful as well!" Kalea turned as Kelsey walked up to her. "And you must be Kelsey." Kelsey nodded her head. "Yes, ma'am I am. It's very nice to meet you Kalea." Kalea smiled and reached in for a hug. The two had an awkward hug and Daxton shrugged his shoulders at Skyler as she looked at him. "Thank you Kalea, now this is Liam and Scott as well. Liam is Kelsey's new fiancé. Now let's have a seat and relax a little!" "Well congratulations to you both and it was very nice to meet you all. I hope we can spend some time together while you are here." Kalea said her goodbyes and headed back behind the restaurant bar. "Nice Dad...." Skyler rolled her eyes at Daxton and he shook his head.

Another young woman came over and then escorted the rest of the group to a table in the corner. "Still the same table, Dax?" "Yes ma'am, that will work for us. They took their seats and had a few seconds of awkward silence before Liam slowly pushed a manila envelope across the cigarette-burned wooden table toward Daxton. "I have heard you are a get-right-to-the-point type of man, Daxton. So here is some information we can discuss further after you get a chance to review it this evening. We can meet at breakfast and go over the details."

Daxton took the envelope folded it in half and stuffed it into his back pocket. Liam looked a bit in shock as he knew that Daxton obviously had no idea what the contents held.

Daxton walked over to Liam and grabbed him by the arm. "Hey bud, you got a couple of minutes to talk outside before our food comes out? "Liam smiled and nodded his head. "Absolutely Mr. Shaw. Shall we?" He raised his hand and pointed to the back deck of the restaurant. The two made their way outside and Daxton turned to Liam. "Let's cut the shit here Liam, you didn't come down here for a visit or for a guided trip. We are both men here so just tell me why you are here and why you drug Kelsey and Skyler down here with you." Liam smiled briefly. "Kelsey said you were a to-the-point kind of man. I respect that." Liam pointed to a high table in the corner. "Let's sit for a moment shall we?" Daxton pulled out a chair and sat down at the table.

"Mr.Shaw I have been working on a very highly regarded project which includes some pieces of art that are almost to the point of being the most valued on the earth. I am a trader of sorts, I am also a collector. I have done my research on you and I find that you are amongst the best when it comes to captaining a ship as well as locating things." Daxton pulled out the envelope and placed it on the table. "I also do my research and I know you are nothing but a glorified thief. I'm going to say whatever is in this envelope will just solidify my theory and it's not about a guided fishing trip." Liam smirked. "You are correct in that aspect. I chose you for a few reasons, you came highly regarded, you are completely washed up, you're a drunk, you have no money and you need money to continue to pay for Skyler's school. You also are familiar with the area and the local islands. You are hiding down here because you cannot face reality but you want to do better and be better. I have that chance right here for you. To be better, to have the finances you would never have dreamed of. To get your life back, your life with your daughter." Daxton sat back in his chair and was silent for a few Moments. "Being a washed-up drunk pilot isn't so bad, but not seeing my daughter grow up kills me."

Liam pushed the envelope back towards Daxton. "This is your ticket to change it all Mr. Shaw. All that I ask is that you review the information and you can let me know what you think tomorrow. If you're not interested then I can locate another captain. It's as simple as that. Now let's go enjoy a drink and get back to the others." Liam winked at Daxton as he got up from his chair. Daxton was curious and wanted to say more but he didn't want to prolong the conversation. "Okay Liam, you have my attention. I will take a look tonight and let you know. Daxton picked up the envelope and placed it into his back pocket. "Thank you, Mr.Shaw, much appreciated. Now let's go have a drink and enjoy the remainder of our evening."

Daxton waved to the waitress as they walked back into the restaurant. At the same time, two gentlemen walked into the front of the restaurant. They caught Daxtons eye instantly and he knew they didn't belong, not local, not tourists.

He looked at Liam, "Those cats with you?"

Liam looked at them and nodded his head slowly, no Mr. Shaw they are not with me.

CHAPTER TWELVE

Daxton peered closely at the map and ran his fingers slowly over a section of the island. There was a shaded red section on the west end that indicated a very rocky region. He was staring at the map as his phone began buzzing on the table indicating he had an incoming call. He picked up the phone and smirked a bit before he hit the answer button. "Mr. Parks Leslie, I didn't figure you'd even call me back what with you being a big shot and all these days."

Parks kicked his boots up on the presidential-style desk that sat in the corner of the warehouse. "Shaw! What the hell are you up to buddy? Damm, it's been a while huh!?"

"It's been way too long my friend! First off, I want to congratulate you on your new show. It's truly awesome to watch you succeed!"

"Well, you can thank Taylor for that. I wanted nothing to do with a TV show, but she pushed and pushed so here we are." So, what's going on these days, heard you were down in Mexico somewhere running charters and flying some again."

"Yessir, in the blood Parks. You know how it is. Just trying to survive and get the blood flowing every now and then."

"I get that dude, so what gives me the pleasure of speaking to Daxton Shaw these days?"

Daxton was quiet for a Moment and wondered if he should just bring up something else. "Palm Island. Know anything about it?"

Parks laughed a little. "Talking about the Palm Island down there in your neck of the woods?"

"Yessir, that's the one," Daxton answered.

Basically, the half-square mile island that sits off the coast of Tecapan? The one that's even hard to locate on a chart or map? The island full of snakes and the waters full of sharks?" Parks asked Daxton

"That's the one Parks," Daxton told him.

"Well, Dax, just off the cuff I know that there was a treasure trove supposedly buried or concealed on the island. It was said that it was jewels and gold brought down from Mazatlán in the early 1800's. The treasure is much older than that. The guys who located it had no way to get it back, so they moved it over to Palm Island. No idea how they located that island, but they did. Taylor and I went down there kind of as a getaway and just to poke around."

"No shit Parks? You were down here? How long ago? Daxton wanted to know.

"Dax, it's been quite a few years ago but we did, that north side is a rocky ass mess, but we had some beautiful dives, gets deep, pretty quickly right off the rocks. Pretty sharky like I said as well and I don't think they see many people in the waters there."

"We spent a few days on the boat making some dives and trips to land, but we didn't have much to go on. But honestly, we drank more wine and relaxed more than we hunted. Anyway, on day three a boat full of militants boarded our boat and tore it apart. Honestly, I thought it would have been worse, but they let us go and told us if we came back, they would just blow us up next time. Needless to say, we didn't make a trip back. I've been blown up before and I swore I wouldn't let that happen again!" Parks joked.

"Yeah, I could see that, Parks." Daxton laughed out loud. Well, I've been asked to locate something that disappeared off the coastline of Palm."

Parks said "Can I ask if are working for someone, treasure hunters? Locals?" Daxton got quiet again before he answered.

"Truth is it's for an international distributor." Parks thought about it for a bit. "Liam Castano?" Daxton was completely surprised that he instantly knew who it was.

"How the hell did you know that, Parks?'

"Unfortunately, Dax, when you do what I do for a living you learn all the shippers, distributors, and pirates on the black market, besides, someone from his offices called here a week or so ago asking if we were for hire for charter trips. I'm not in that game and I'm not a fan of his in the slightest. Never called the dude back. Obviously, he's shopping for someone to help him out with something over there."

Daxton told him "That's my ex-wife's new fiancé."

"Oh, shit Daxton. I had no idea, sorry to hear that but if you can talk her out of it as a friend, I would highly recommend it."

"Note taken Parks, kinda gathered that anyway,"

"So, what else are you looking for Dax? Anything else I can help you with?"

Daxton answered, "Man, not really. Just wanted to pick your brain a bit to see if there's anything I should know before I bit this off. I trust you and I knew that you would have some input for me brother."

"Yeah, watch your back It's not the sharks in the waters I would worry about. If Liam is looking for something I can tell you that others are already on it as well." Park's son, Stan came running up and grabbed him around the upper leg. "C'mon, Dad let's go. Mommy said you would take all day and for me to come and get you." Parks rubbed his son's head.

"Go dude, go be with your family buddy and it was great to catch up. One day we'll make that beer happen that we always lie about to each other."

Parks laughed as Stan drug on his pants leg, "Absolutely, comrade, tell you what. I know I made a file for Palm so let me dig it up when I get a chance."

"Sounds great Parks and thanks again for calling me back."

"Anytime, Dax, and same here. Good to hear your voice. Take care of yourself down there and just be really careful who you trust."

CHAPTER THIRTEEN

The weights in the gym clanged together, and you could hear the treadmills singing as everyone got their workouts in. Daxton slid the forty-five-pound weight on the end of the bar one by one. He hadn't touched a weight in over a year, but he wanted to see where his strength level was. He threw some light reps in just to dust the cobwebs off his joints and added a few more plates to the bar. His newly found friend, Scott reached over for a 25 and slid it on his side. "Let's stay at 225 for a few reps boss.

"You trying to hurt yourself boss?'

Daxton winked at Scott and loaded one more plate onto the bar saying, "Man, I have been hurting for two years. Let's see how hard I can hurt physically now. You better act like I'm gettin' this shit up even if I can't. I know most of these people here".

Scott chuckled and slapped Daxton on the back. "Tell you what, I got you if you tell me why you're so fucked up. I've been around your ex-wife if that's what she is, and I only hear one side. We're all a little fucked up after what we've been through. It's okay to talk about it boss."

Daxton sat on the bench and looked up at Scott. "Tell you what, If I hit this without you touching the bar, I'll tell you about it. How's that for a deal?"

A young woman walked by as Daxton was lying back on the bench, "Hey, Dax, what the heck are you doing in here? We haven't seen you in like a year. This is a different kind of bar for you, right?" Daxton shook his head.

"Thanks for calling me back about that free dive trip you said you were taking me on." She jokingly slapped him on the leg with her towel. "I'm kidding, glad to see you in here." The woman walked away, and Scott looked down at Daxton.

"Obviously during your hurting phase, you made some really

nice friends' boss.". Daxton laid back down on the bench.

"That's enough of the boss BS he told Scott. We are equals, got that?"

"Sure boss, just get this weight up!" Scott replied.

Daxton slapped his hands together and then placed them on the cold rigid steel bar. He took one more deep breath and dropped the weight onto his chest. "Holy shit, this is heavy." He thought to himself as he pushed the weight up his arms and began to shake.

"C'mon boss, get that shit up! Let's get it!" Scott yelled as Daxton struggled with the lift. Daxton channeled his thoughts, clenched his jaw, and pushed as hard as he could. Scott's hands were underneath the bar as it inched further and further up.

He heard another "c'mon boss" from Scott as he let out a yell and pushed the bar all the way up and back into the rack.

He jumped up off the bench and Eric grabbed him and patted his back. "That's the ticket, son. You still got that fire in you.!"

Daxton put his hands on the bench and took a deep breath.

"Damn, that's a lot heavier than it used to be!" They both laughed as they began unloading plates from the bar.

"Looks like we got some talking to do now, doesn't it?"

Daxton shook his head up and down indicating yes.

"You know what Scott? I'm a man of my word and maybe it will do some good to talk about it a little bit, right?" Scott wiped off the bench and threw Daxton his towel.

"Damn straight it will help".

"But now I have a question for you big guy. How in the hell did you get hooked up with a guy like Liam and why?" As Scott unloaded the weights from the bar he looked at Daxton. "You know sometimes we go through some shit in life where you don't get a lot of options. And the ones presented to you at that time come in a rare form. Maybe not how you wanted it, or what you wanted but it just seems to work out. I mean not far from what just happened to you." He winked at Daxton. "I was broke as a joke and needed the money. I had a skillset that Liam was looking for so he made me an offer I couldn't pass up."

The gym owner approached Daxton. "Hey, dude, if you keep showing up, I'll comp your membership". Military discount ya know".

Daxton shook his hand as he replied. "I really appreciate that brother, I don't need the discount, just serving my country was enough. You give that discount to that kid over there working his ass off. How about that?" The gym owner smiled and said," You got a deal, but your ass better show up here for workouts or I'll throw him out".

Daxton told him, "You got a deal!"

Then he asked Daxton," Who's your silver-back gorilla friend here?

Daxton grabbed Scott's giant arm. "This is Scott, he's an old Corp buddy of mine."

"I say it's always good to have friends like you buddy." He said shaking Scott's hand.

As he was walking toward his office he turned and said,

"Good to see you, Dax, the door is always open for you and your friend," and headed back to his office.

Scott and Daxton made their way out of the gym and headed for the Jeep.

"Well, I guess you're not going to let me off so let's go grab a bite to eat and we can talk about it all. I'm glad we met up, totally jacked up circumstances but nonetheless glad we did."

Scott said," Couldn't agree more boss. It's not every day you meet someone that totally understands you or is like-minded anymore."

Daxton replied," No kidding there, they just don't make 'em' like us anymore!"

They acted as if they had been lifelong friends and they each talked about the places they had been as Daxton fired up the Jeep and they headed out to grab lunch.

CHAPTER FOURTEEN

Liam and Mateo both stood on the makeshift pier and scaffolding that flanked the submarine. The sub was supported by wooden saddles down in the twenty-foot trench that had been excavated for its assembly. "Well, is this thing going to work as well as you say, Mateo? Damn thing better for what it cost me."

"Yeah, it'll work. This is our test run so I'm sure as always, we will have kinks to work out before it sets sail on its actual mission."

Liam lit up another cigarette, pulled a deep drag off it, and blew smoke into the air. "I know you don't want to know what the payload is for the submarine, but I need you to know that it is world-life-altering and needs to be as secure as possible Mateo."

Mateo shook his head in agreement. "It is. Best I have assisted in design and construction to date." One of the men hit a large button on the wall and the sub started to rise into the air slowly. The sub was glossy blue that you could almost look through, with perfect lines on the body and amazingly sleek.

Liam's eyes lit up as the sub slowly came into view. He started clapping and looking at the others in the group telling them "She is a work of art if anything!"

"Okay, guys. That's far enough." Mateo told the worker.

The man let go of the button and the submarine stopped elevating. "Hey, Mateo, are you a green light to start letting water in? All systems go before we dunk her?" he asked.

Mateo responded with enthusiasm. "Yes Sir! Everything has been looked over multiple times and we are good to go!"

Alright guys, let's flood it." One of the men pulled the lever down that controlled the coffer dam. The dam gates began to open, and the water sprayed through the cracks until it opened larger, and a huge amount of water rushed in. It filled the basin in a matter of a few seconds. The construction basin was built next to a river making it easy access to the ocean. The rushing water settled into the basin and Mateo took one more walk around for close inspection finally telling the workers

"She's good. He waved at the controller and the man hit the button. The slender submarine was being lowered into the water. The coffer dam gate was now fully open, and the vessel was fully submerged. Mateo went to the workbench and flipped the latch on the large pelican waterproof case.

The case was the main operating unit. It consisted of a large monitor, gauges, and dials to control the sub. Mateo turned the unit on and all the instruments lit up. He carefully checked all of the readings and then pulled out the controller.

Liam walked over closer to Mateo and looked over his shoulder. "Millions of dollars and you are going to use a video game controller to drive my submarine?"

Mateo brushed off Liam's comment and turned on the split-screen monitor. He adjusted a few things and fired the propellors. The submarine rotated ninety degrees towards the opening that followed the river. He added some power and the sub slowly moved through the gates. A small dimly lit boat pulled up along the sub and radioed to Mateo. "We are in place and ready to follow her out.

Mateo pushed to power higher, and the sub started clipping along at a few more knots. The boat stayed close to the sub until it was closer to the ocean. As the boat peeled off and turned around Mateo dropped the submarine five feet below the surface of the water. All functions were operating as designed with no issues. The moonlight danced on the rippled water that the sub displaced as it headed out to sea on its maiden voyage.

CHAPTER FIFTEEN

Daxton walked through the front of the five-star resort in his ripped-up baggie shorts and a Pacifico Beer tank top and was met with an "Excuse me, sir, are you staying with us?" Irritated, Daxton abruptly replied, "Do I look like the kinda guy that stays in a place like this lady? I'm trying to find my family and a friend. He said they were by the pool."

"Well, you're not allowed to walk around the premises without being accompanied by a guest of the hotel," she replied.

"Look lady, I don't want to be here either! I just want to …."

Liam walked into the hallway donning his black Speedo, hands in the air. "Daxton, my friend, please join us out at the pool for a cocktail. He is with me, add Daxton Shaw to the guest list.", he said to the desk clerk. "I am sorry Mr. Castano. I will add him to the list now."

"I'm good, dude and that's a nice banana hammock you got there, Liam. It's even shiney man, very well done."

"You know I try my best when I can," Liam laughed saying, follow me, we are back here in the corner."

As Daxton walked closer to the pool cabana, he could see Kelsey and Skyler both in bathing suits, reading.

Kelsey, you are obviously not missing any workouts these days, he thought to himself. When he walked into their view Skyler threw her book down on the layout chair and jumped up.

"Daddy, you came! Very surprising." She hugged his neck and kissed his cheek.

"You own a real bathing suit Sky? Jesus, I don't know if yours or Liam's is worse!" She laughed and grabbing his hand said, "C'mon, let's go talk to Mom".

Liam motioned for the waiter. "Excuse me, can you get this man a drink? Daxton, tell him what you want."

The man looked at Daxton and grabbed his notepad.

Daxton thought about it for a second and just ordered a double Topo Chico on ice with lime. Kelsey looked over the top of her sunglasses at Daxton and he smiled at her just as Scott walked over.

"Heya Boss, how ya feeling after the gym? Daxton shook his hand and gave him a bro hug. Then he whispered closer to Scott's ear. "I almost couldn't get out of bed." Then he pulled back and spoke loud enough for the other to hear.

"All good bud, that was just an easy version of what I used to do." He winked at Scott and turned back to the others.

"You sure you don't want a drink, Mr. Shaw?" Liam asked.

"Pretty sure I'll be happy with the one I just ordered Liam but thank you. And your balls are falling out."

Liam looked down and looked back up at Daxton.

"You are the joker aren't you, Mr. Shaw." Liam couldn't help but laugh a bit before he was ready to get down to business. He got his laptop out of its case and Daxton walked away to give him time to get set up. He walked by Kelsey as he headed for the shady area. "Hey Kels, nice bathing suit. You get a half-off sale on those that thing hopefully"?

"Hey Dax, glad to see you still have the tact and charm you've always had, you will never change." she replied.

Daxton winked at her and slowly walked back to where Liam was setting up his laptop. As he approached Liam he asked, "How many days are we going to lay low on this Liam? I canceled all my charters and I'm going to go broke just sitting here." Liam turned on his computer and faced the screen so Daxton could see it.

"Well Mr. Shaw, that's why I wanted to visit with you today. Everyone is pulling out of the area that we are concerned about. No one has been around the island in over twenty-four hours so things are settling, and I think we should make plans for the retrieval."

Daxton watched the footage and the map on the laptop telling Liam, "The weather will be most cooperative in about two days from now. It's going to be too choppy until then. So, can we shoot for then?" Liam nodded his head, "I trust your judgment Daxton. What else will we need for our journey? I have the list and all of it secured."

Daxton sat down in the chair as the waiter handed him his drink. "I'm bringing the main gear, just make sure the boat is gassed up. Also, Scott is with us. Can I have access to the boat this evening? I want to check to see what she has onboard."

Liam told Daxton that was not a problem, and that he would inform the crew at the docks that he would be down to board the boat later.

Skyler came over to the table where they sat. "What can I do to help Dad?" she asked.

Daxton took a sip of his drink. "You're diving with me Sky; we're going down together. And looking over at Liam he added, I don't want anyone else on our initial dive," Liam shook his head in understanding, telling Daxton "You are running this operation, Mr. Shaw." Skyler smiled with delight. "I want to look at your gear Dad, I don't trust your janky ass old stuff."

"You need to calm down kiddo, my stuff has hit depths yours can't even touch."

"You haven't been around in a while, and I've already matched and surpassed your depths sucker! I sent you a text, but I guess you don't remember."

Daxton knew she was right and felt bad and proud at the same time. "I remember Sky and you're not a little girl anymore. Hell, you've probably already logged more dives than I did by the time I was forty. Anyway, yes, we'll do a complete gear check tomorrow sweetheart." Skyler smiled and said, "Deal!"

"Anyhow, I think we have everything we need, and if I come up with anything else I'll call or have Scott get in touch with you. Let me look at the times that would be best to leave when it gets a little closer."

Liam nodded in agreement. "That sounds perfect Mr. Shaw, we will await your call on the timing. If you need to be paid for your wait time, I can accommodate you on that as well." Liam told him.

"I am good, Liam. I appreciate it but I am okay. I just want to spend a little time with my daughter while I have her down here."

Skyler smiled again and Liam nodded, saying "Absolutely understandable. You two enjoy your time and if you need anything please allow me to assist."

Kelsey had her sunglasses on but had been watching and listening to them. She did still love Daxton and somehow, she could see that a little bit of him had come back to life and back to the man she fell in love with. Skyler and Daxton walked by Kelsey. Daxton pulled his shades down and winked once again. "You have a good time now ya hear? I'll be on the lookout for the rest of that bathing suit!" he teased. Kelsey and Skyler both laughed. "I'll bring Sky back later tonight. We have some catching up to do. I will text you if we are later than we think Mom." Skyler added.

"Okay, Sky. Daxton, you take care of her." Kelsey knew she didn't need to say it. He had guarded and protected their daughter from all things since the day Skyler came into the world.

Daxton threw the peace signal into the air without looking back as he and Skyler made their way out of the hotel.

CHAPTER SIXTEEN

Kelsey walked over to the enormous four-poster bedside and rested her hand over the top of Mrs. Castano's hand. "Try to get some rest Miriam, you are going to need it for your upcoming lady's night!" Miriam smiled and reached over and squeezed Kelsey's hand.

"You know Kelsey, I always enjoy getting out, but I mostly always enjoy your company and the stories you tell me I feel like you're the daughter I was never given."

Ever since Daxton went south, Kelsey had to revert to home health nursing for the extra money. It wasn't that she didn't enjoy the work, but she missed her old life terribly. Kelsey smiled from ear to ear. "Thank you, Miriam, I feel like we've built such a strong relationship and I love our time together and our talks. But trust me, I gave my own mother a real run for her money. Let's just say you get the best years with me."

Miriam smiled, then chuckled and slowly closed her eyes.

"Okay gorgeous, I'm going to head out now so you can rest. I will see you again tomorrow and sneak you in another one of those sugar cookies you like." Kelsey smiled at Miriam and quietly headed out of her room. As she closed the door of the bedroom Miriam's son, Liam approached her.

"Good day, Mrs. Shaw, can we speak for a Moment in the dining room before you leave today?"

Kelsey nodded and followed him toward the dining room. She could not imagine what Liam wanted to talk to her about. They finally made their way to the dining room after walking through the grandiose mansion hallways.

"Mrs. Shaw, I want to say thank you for your patience and giving kind nature towards my mother. She values you like a family member, and I can never repay you for that. But there is one thing I would like to ask you. I watch you; you are an amazing person and very beautiful. I would love to have the opportunity to take you …."

Kelsey stopped Liam in mid-sentence. "Mr. Castano, I am flattered but it's just not a good time in my life right now. I am raising my teenage daughter, working two jobs, and taking care of myself."

Liam stepped a little closer to Kelsey. "This is why I ask you; I can see you need help, someone to care for you as you care for others. I will not take no for an answer, but I will tell you what. Let's start with coffee maybe next week and just go from there. Now what would you say to that?"

Kelsey took a deep breath and beyond her better judgment she agreed. "Okay, but just coffee."

Liam smiled with delight and snapped his fingers. "You have a deal, Mrs. Shaw, just a coffee. I will have my staff get your schedule and pick you up when you are available next week."

Kelsey smirked a little and regretted her decision already. She shook her head lightly. "Okay, Mr. Castano, we will see you then. I need to get going to my appointment now."

As Kelsey made her way through the twelve-foot-tall double doors Liam yelled at her. "Oh, and Mrs. Shaw, please call me Liam from now on. I would like us to be casual. Mr. Castano is just too stuffy!"

Kelsey smiled and shook her head yes as she was slowly closing the large door behind her.

CHAPTER SEVENTEEN

Liam Castano was raised until the age of fourteen in Cuba. His parents were considered middle class, but they wanted more for their only son. He excelled in school and was a favored personality amongst his classmates even being so young. Everyone wanted to be his friend.

He was flashy, watched American rockstars, rappers , and kept up with moguls that were making millions in the United States.

Liam wanted that and he knew he could make it. He mimicked all the idols he watched on TV through the years.

The young motivated boy started a business at the age of twelve, selling four-day-old bread and cookies that he bought from the bakery and sold to rich kids for double what the bakery charged. He found he had a knack for selling. He learned to read people and manipulated them to his advantage.

When Liam turned fourteen after years of telling his parents he wanted to move to the U.S. they realized it was time. Liam had an uncle who was very successful in the trade business and lived in Miami. His parents made the decision that it was best for him to go to learn from his uncle. There wasn't much opportunity to flourish as a young man in Cuba with his talent. Liam's parents put him on a plane to Mexico City where his uncle met him to accompany him to the U.S. and his new home in Miami.

Liam stayed under the radar and never enrolled in school. His schooling came from his uncle and his uncle's employees. He learned math calculations, shipping business management, and how to keep his mouth shut. The business was for the Castano family. Liam's uncle shipped everything from twenty pounds of avocados to a thousand pounds of Xanax. Liam soaked it all in and learned geography in a different way than most. When he worked doing shipping details, he always looked at the map because he was interested in where the goods would end up. He made a list of the places he wanted to visit as he learned as much as possible about the places he shipped to.

As Liam got older, he was given free rein to secure customers. His dreams of living the lifestyle he idolized were coming true. He found his way into the Miami lifestyle rather quickly and rubbed shoulders with promoters, rockstars, moguls, rappers, and drug dealers. He had made it. He could walk into any place in Miami. He was invited to all the large events.

He had connections to clothing companies, startups, exotic cars, real estate, and goods. He considered all the other stuff "flashy" but he knew that "goods' were where the money was made. He would take 20k and turn it into 500k take his cut and make the same deals four to five times a week. This way of doing business grew for Liam and he had enough money to be set for life. But for Liam, it was never enough. He wanted more. He wanted the "Big Leagues" and to help the little guys. Weapons, war shipping, providing weapons for small countries and cities to protect themselves from Communism or being overrun by their own countries.

Liam found his connections eventually into the weapons game, but he started small, he learned the ropes as to how to get around the red tape in selling and shipping firearms and ammunition. He shipped weapons all over the world. It started with a pallet here and a pallet there, then came the large orders and it became cargo containers full, one container, then three, then seventeen. He was overrun with orders and was known for being able to come through with orders that others could not fill.

Unfortunately, being in the weapons business came with a price. Liam had witnessed lies, shady deals, questionable individuals, and even murder along the way. He always tried to keep his head down but after a time he became callous to the dirty world around him. He had lost his way, he was now a changed man because of the world he was immersed in.

After three solid weeks of working almost fifteen-hour days, Liam was breaking down. He needed to get away. He loved his exotic and antique cars and decided he needed to just drive and get away for a few days. He packed a bag loaded it into his 1973 Corvette Stingray and headed toward the Keys.

Liam arrived in the Keys around sunset that Sunday evening. He pulled up to the quaint hotel that was owned by one of his customers. He got out of the car and tossed the valet driver the keys.

"Will you be needing your vehicle this evening Mr. Castano?"the valet asked as Liam reached in and grabbed his bag. Liam could tell the young valet driver was Cuban and he walked over to him, pulled out his wallet, pulled out two hundred dollars cash, and stuffed it into the young man's front pocket. "Not tonight, my young friend, not tonight." The young man's face lit up and he happily got into the Corvette while Liam walked through the front entrance.

"Good evening Mr. Castano. It's been several years since you have made it back to visit us!"

Liam smirked as the clerk slid the room key across the desk.

"It has been much too long." When Liam started getting notoriety, he frequented the Keys often, many of his clients including the one who owned this hotel, would go down to get away from the Miami scene and relax from time to time.

Liam fit in well with the upper class and the super-rich. People admired his story and his grit in the business world.

He opened the door to his suite and threw his bag on the bed. Typically, he would have others taking care of every detail of his trips, but he didn't want that this time. He wanted to get away for a while. Not worry about work or having to keep up his business persona. He changed into a pair of shorts and a T-shirt and headed out the door.

CHAPTER EIGHTEEN

The cars and motorcycles raced only feet away from the cantina tables that were on the dirty sidewalk. The owner of the small cantina constantly sliced from the large spinning top of meat for the patrons waiting for tacos. He yelled the names of the customers as he finished putting the tacos together and passed them out as fast as he could. He smiled as Daxton and Skyler walked by. "Mr. Shaw! My dearest friend in the world! I know you can't walk by without having tacos and a beer!" he said in broken English. Skyler smiled knowing it was not hard to love her father, not just her but everyone around him. He had his problems, but his soul and personality were gigantic. "I'm actually pretty hungry Dad. Let's get a taco." She winked at her Dad, he put his arm around her shoulder and kissed her head.

"You've always had my appetite Sky. Your Mom never could figure out where you put it all.

"Maybe she doesn't understand because she eats like a damn bird!" They were both laughing as they stepped into line for fresh tacos. "So, how do you like living down here and what do you do for fun these days? Never get many dive pictures from you anymore. Just sayin'."

Daxton rolled his eyes knowing what his daughter was getting at. "Well, lately I've been working a lot paying for your damn tuition!" He laughed as she punched him in the shoulder.

"You know I give two shits about school and rather you be home and save your money. That's on you and Mom for the whole degree thing, totally worthless." She stuck her tongue out at him as they got to the front of the line to the Al Pastor.

"Hey buddy, you have a new woman in your life I see ehhh? She is a ten! A beautiful ten Especially for you!" He laughed as one of his waiters brought two beers garnished with limes. "Here you go Mr. Dax and one for the lady friend as well." Daxton grabbed the beers and Skyler yanked one out of his hand. He looked down at her and gave her a look she recognized well. "Don't even come at me, Dad. I've been drinking beer since I had a bottle, and you know it."

"Yea, but not drinkin' drinkin. I've seen you slam about ten since you have been here!" he said.

"Do you really want to start a lecture or just have some tacos and enjoy our time?" Skyler questioned.

Daxton wanted to give the Dad talk but she was right. He had no room to talk, and he did want to spend quality time with her as much as he could. He reminded himself that she was growing up and coming into her own. She wasn't his "little girl" anymore. She was figuring out the world on her own and it crushed his soul knowing he was missing so much of it.

She clanged her beer to his. "Cheers, Daddy, I love you, and thank you for letting them finally bring me down here."

"Cheers, love and you're welcome!" he replied.

He looked at the man who was shaving the Al Pastor and addressed him. "She's my daughter, Jesus!"

Jesus yelled back at him as he handed Daxton the four tacos.

"Well, she is still a ten but just in a different way senior! I don't want to get beat up by Mr. Dax! On the house and welcome to you my city young lady!" he told Skyler. He kissed her cheek in welcome as Daxton found them a table.

"You know we all miss you at home don't you Dad? I mean people still ask about you at the grocery store, church, every single place we go." Skyler took a huge bite of her taco.

"Jesus, these are amazing!" she said between bites.

"Speaking of church! Easy, Sky, easy, but you are right they are the best!"

They sat at the small cantina table enjoying their time eating, laughing, and talking. Daxton noticed two men come into the cantina.

"You know Dad, Mom probably misses you the most. She had too many glasses of wine one night and she told me how she cries herself to sleep and how much she still loves you."

Daxton shook his head as he was watching the men and listening to Skyler. "What? That's horrible! I mean, ughhh, you know what I mean. I hate that for your mother. Look, put a pin in this. We have some company Sky.

You remember the two guys that walked into the restaurant last night that I was eyeballing?" Skyler shook her head yes.

"Well, it looks like they didn't get enough of us last night, guessing they just want an old-fashioned meet and greet. Follow my lead, kick the shit out of the leg on one of their chairs, we do it all the time to each other and it works every time. I will get the other and when I say go, get your ass to the Jeep. Got it Sky?" She nervously nodded, "You sure Dad? Should we wait for the others?"

Daxton told her, "No, they aren't going to wait or give us much time. We got this baby. Keep it together." Her Dad had said that to her thousands of times over the years. "Keep it together" It calmed her soul instantly and she knew she would be okay as her Dad was her ultimate protector.

Daxton looked straight at both men as he walked toward them. He raised his voice, meaning to cause a scene. He knew if something happened, he wanted many eyes to observe.

"Why, hello gentlemen! We've been watching you watch us for two days now and we just can't stand it anymore. We must introduce ourselves." He held out his hand to shake hands with one of them. They looked at each other in confusion as Skyler got closer to one of their chairs.

"That's fine guys, not everyone possesses that good ol' southern hospitality like we do." He winked at Sky and at the exact same time they kicked the front legs from the plastic chairs. Just as Daxton said, the chair legs exploded and both of me came down with them.

"Go!" Daxton yelled and they both ran toward the Jeep. "Don't look back Sky, just run. We have a good lead so far."

As they ran through the crowded square they pushed and bumped into people as they sprinted their way across the sea of people in the parking lot.

"What do they want Dad?"

Daxton yelled to Skyler. "Just Go! Talk later!" he said breathing heavily."

The men started pushing their way through the crowd in pursuit of Daxton and Skyler. One of them caught sight of them running and yelled to his partner. "There they go!"

Skyler jumped into the driver's seat of the Jeep and Daxton yelled, "No ma'am! Move, that's my spot!"

There's no time Dad, get in now!" Skyler turned on the ignition and the Jeep fired up. Daxton saw the two men closing in fast, so he jumped in the backseat. Skyler slammed the Jeep in reverse and hit one of the men as she twisted the steering wheel around. The other man grabbed hold of the Jeep's bumper but could not hang on as she sped away. Both men sprang up and dusted themselves off as a black SUV sled to a stop and they jumped in telling the driver to "Go!"

Skyler straightened up the rear-view mirror and watched the men get into the SUV. "Dad, they aren't done yet. They just got into an SUV and are following!"

Daxton picked himself up off the floorboard and looked over the backseat. Then he crawled over into the passenger's seat. "Okay, Sky, listen to me. If we can make it out of town, we're in the clear. Take a left just up there," he said pointing out the way,

Skyler dodged around a car and made a hard left. "Okay, now why in the hell are they after us Dad? Tell me now!" Daxton looked behind them.

"They want what I have Sky, it's what Liam brought to me. It's information on the location of a sunken submarine that has something in it that they all want. Liam isn't down here for a rich man's guided fishing trip. He came down here to hire me to get whatever the hell is in that sub."

"Well, what the hell is it?!"

"I have no damn clue, Sky, honestly. Turn right here!"

The Jeep turned right as the black SUV slid into the side of them. The collision was loud and violent. Skyler screamed but held on tight to the wheel. One of the men rolled down his window and aimed his pistol at Daxton but before he could get a good aim Skyler rammed them back as the man fired and missed. "Turn right there!"

The Jeep slid sideways as she turned to the right, but the SUV swung out too hard and couldn't make the turn. The Jeep made some distance and Daxton and Skyler were screaming at each other.

"Okay, okay! Sky, take the next left and that's going to get us out of town!"

"Where is your gun Dad? You always have a gun!" Skyler yelled.

"Not down here, haven't needed one until now!" Daxton dug through the center console and finding nothing he dropped the cover on the glovebox and reached in. He pulled out a flare gun. "Gonna have to make do, sweetheart."

As they made their way through the outskirts of the city they managed to calm down. "Okay, Sky, I think we managed to......" Daxton hadn't finished his sentence before the black SUV pulled directly in front of them at an intersection. Daxton looked at Skyler as the passenger rolled down the window. Skyler looked at the flare gun in Daxton's lap.

"When I take the shot...." He cocked the pistol. "Turn right up ahead and just drive!" He jumped out of the Jeep and aimed the pistol toward the front window opening. The SUV driver flinched as he saw the flare leave the gun. It went directly into the window and bounced around the inside of the vehicle. The light was blinding, and the flare burned them as it bounced back and forth.

Seeing that the flare had done its job, Daxton ran back to the Jeep and Skyler hit the gas.

The men in the SUV jumped out and watched the Jeep kick up dust as it sped away on the dirt road headed to the coastline.

CHAPTER NINETEEN

The lightning crashed off in the distance as the helicopter came to rest again in the wet soil of the jungle. The side door to the black chopper slid open and two men jumped out. As their boots hit the mud, they pulled the black waterproof case from the floor of the helicopter and headed for the warehouse. The two guards standing at the building opened the door and all the men stepped inside. Mateo examined the case.

"Same weight as we discussed, correct?" Liam walked over and placed his hand on the case.

"To the ounce. And to the size, no alterations." Mateo had built the cargo area of the sub exactly the size of the case.

Liam leaned in and looked at Mateo. "I will say this once again. What is in this case is priceless for many more reasons than you will ever understand. This CANNOT be lost. Do you understand?" Liam said in a harsh tone.

"I do not ask or care what is in this case. You asked me to build a sub that can handle this job. And that I did. It will NOT be lost!" Mateo said as he ran his hand over the case.

"We need to load this now and get out of the river." Liam motioned for the two men to move the case to the submarine. Mateo joined them at the sub and showed them the specific area that the case was to be loaded into.

"Place it in here. This area will also be sealed in case of a breach. Whatever is in your case will be protected by a backup." he said as Liam watched the process.

The men slid the case into the perfectly sized safe box located in the hull of the submarine. Mateo closed the hatch on the area and turned the knob on the top. The latch locked into place and sealed the contents shut. "Okay, she is ready to be tightened up now." Mateo stepped off the edge of the submarine and the workers came to the edge to tighten the main deck screws. "We will be ready to sail the ship in fifteen minutes. Let's flood the gates and get her up and going." The men scrambled as Mateo opened the control case. The area flooded and submerged the submarine-like it had done the two previous trials prior. The warehouse was empty. All the tools, drawings, and contents were removed. Mateo fired up all the controls and looked at Liam. "Once we get her clear of the inlet we go." Liam twirled his finger in the air and ordered his men back to the helicopter telling Mateo "We will have the helicopter ready to relocate."

Mateo remotely guided the submarine on track down the river. He was pleased that everything was working perfectly as he had designed it to do. As the sub cleared the river inlet Mateo placed the sub on course, closed the case, and gave his workers a satisfied nod. As he walked out the men poured fuel on the edges of the makeshift warehouse. He threw the case inside of the helicopter and closed the door behind him.

The pilot slowly lifted the helicopter into the air as lightning still struck off in the distance. As the chopper gained altitude, Mateo looked back down to where he had spent months working on his project. The building erupted into a huge fireball that was sent hundreds of feet into the air. As the mushroom cloud rolled on itself Mateo knew that this was just the beginning of the chaos that he was about to be in the middle of. Little did he know that it wasn't just himself about to be amid the chaos and life-changing situations.

CHAPTER TWENTY

"How many more hours until we are close to the extraction point?" Liam asked as he stood over the occupied Mateo.

Mateo meticulously monitored all the submarine's readouts on the lit-up screen in front of him. He was so zoned into watching all the gauges he took a minute to answer Liam.

Liam grabbed Mateo by the shoulder and Mateo spun around and grabbed his arm. "I am sorry, I haven't slept in four days, and I just want you to make sure this operation goes well for you Liam. I apologize." He looked back at the monitor. "It says seven hours and forty-seven minutes. Our sub at the location plus or minus half an hour or so depending on underwater currents. We have never pushed her quite that far during the test runs since we didn't have the time." Mateo looked up at Liam.

"Mateo, the contents could no longer sit and wait. People were talking, noise in the background. The industry was speculating and getting close. We had no choice but to get them out of here as soon as we could." Liam lit up a cigarette and put his hand back on Mateo's shoulder. "And besides, I've seen her run six hours without a trace of an issue. I have faith in your design and construction. I've been highly impressed and after this Mateo, I feel that we can make a lot of money in the future." Mateo didn't say anything and only watched his monitor.

Liam continued, "The next two hours the sub will be on autopilot. The course she is on is a straight path, the seas are cooperating and there's no one in the area, apart from a few cargo ships. That will allow us time to get to the next point of contact with her. After that, we get into more congested waters, and I want to oversee her until we get to the mark."

"Do you have faith, Mateo?" Mateo looked back at him, "Yes, I feel like there will be no issues. We have tested...." Liam interrupted him mid-sentence.

"No, do you have faith? Real faith Mateo?" Mateo looked confused for a second, "Yes, yes I do."

"Okay, good. It's always good to have a little faith even if you have luck and skill. Let's throw a little of that faith into play. This will be the biggest and most thought-out transport project that anyone has ever seen. I would like to think that one day we will be talked about. Pioneers of the industry one might even say."

The door swung open, and a man dressed in black tactile clothing looked inside the room. "Boss, the chopper is ready to go when you are. We are leaving two men here to make sure we have not been followed." Liam shook his head and pulled a drag from his cigarette.

"Well Mateo, it looks like our ride is here."

The silent and sleek submarine cut through the waters like a sharp dagger. The hydrodynamics of the hull were designed with such precision that not even a ripple of water displacement could be seen. The moonlight glared on the surface of the ocean.

Mateo took one last glance at the monitor. He checked the speed, the location, the power level, the depth, and the heading. His finger hovered over the autopilot setting before he was ready to activate it. He slowly placed his finger on the button, looked back at Liam, then pushed the button.

"It's time to go. She's all on her own now."

CHAPTER TWENTY ONE

The backside of Palm Island was calm. It glistened as the small boat rocked slightly in the ripples that the ocean sent their way. Circles were popping up as the small rollers came across the rocks that sat below the surface. The pelicans sat in the trees just yards away from the boat. Though she fought in her mind, Skyler broke the silence as they picked up the fishing rods from the rod holsters. "I know you didn't bring me out here to talk about my grades Dad."

Daxton couldn't' help but smile. He knew his daughter was a reader of people. "You always could drag things out of people Sky. I don't know if it's a talent or a curse." Daxton got a piece of cut bait from the box. He picked out an extra and tossed it to Skyler. She caught it and slid the bait onto her hook.

"Well Dad, pretty sure I got that from you, damn sure not from Mom. She can go quiet for a month or not talk to anyone including me."

Daxton took a deep breath as he dropped his line into the water. "It's seventy-five feet deep sweetheart, trigger fish will bump it on the way down the ledge. Don't pull hard on those. Wait until it gets to depth. That's where you want to be." he instructed Skyler.

Skyler clicked her reel off and spooled down.

"Jesus, Dad why can't you just talk to me? It's like since I've grown up you hold it all in. I'm not your little girl anymore and I'm not ever going to be again. Mom cries herself to sleep every night. I've stayed with her; she still loves you and can't understand what she did wrong to make you leave us both." Skyler paused and looked at her Dad. "I'm sorry Dad, that was way too much, I didn't mean to……"

Daxton stopped her in mid-sentence as life drained out of him briefly. "Sky, I didn't leave you or your mother. We didn't see eye to eye anymore and I had more issues that I didn't want her to have to deal with. That was on me. And you were going to college and growing up. That was not the intent and sure not what I ever wanted you to think! I came down here for a job."

A tear ran down Skyler's face as she knew her Dad was telling the truth. But, why so far Dad? You could fly or captain anywhere, but you left!"

Daxton swiveled around in his seat as he wiped a tear from his eye. "One day you will understand kiddo. I love you more than life itself." The emotions broke as Skyler's reel started spinning offline. "Hook up!" Daxton laid his rod down and ran to the back of the boat. "Reel down, Sky, she looks heavy."

The rod bent almost all the way down to the water. The line slowly disappeared off the spool as she held the rod tightly between her legs.

"Dad, it's going to spool me It's going deeper!" Daxton grabbed the lower portion of her rod to feel the tension.

"Yup, whatever is on that line doesn't want to come see us.

She's a heavy girl!" Daxton ran to the center console and got the fighting belt. "Stand up baby! Hold the rod tight first."

Skyler stood up as Daxton wrapped the belt around her waist.

"Okay, Sky, let's see what she's made of. Let's get some line back on that reel" He tightened down the drag slowly as the fight eased. "Don't get comfortable, as soon as she sees the surface it's game on again." Skyler cranked down, then up, then down, then up.

"We have to get her away from the rocks." Daxton hurried to the helm, turned the boat around, and headed off away from the island. "Okay, Sky, we are going to drag her away from the rocks for a bit. Hold tight." The reel spun off and then slowed again.

"You know Mom will always love you, Dad. Quit fighting it."

Daxton turned as he pushed the throttle a little further forward.

"Right now, you need to fight that fish! And she really loves me?" Daxton yelled as he had feelings he hadn't had in a very long time.

"Hell, yeah she does, and this new guy is just a phase. She'll always wait for you to come back!"

Daxton pulled the boat into neutral and returned to the back of the boat. "Sky, I didn't know. I thought I did too much damage."

Skyler reeled down as hard as she could. "I'm done talking about this, let's get this fuckin' fish on the boat!"

Daxton laughed and came to life. "Let's get her baby!"

The two of them fought the fish for the next hour. As it came to the surface, they couldn't believe what had happened. A White Marlin rolled over as if to say just let me go. Daxton tied off the Marlin and Skyler took a quick selfie of them both with the fish. They high-fived and hugged each other, and both started crying. "I love you, Dad. I've missed you."

"I love you too Sky and things will be changing after this I swear. What do you want to do with this beast?"

Skyler kissed her Dad on the cheek and said, "Let her free."

Daxton pulled his knife from his side and cut the line. He slid his hand over the White Marlin as he released it and it slowly disappeared into the abyss.

"We haven't talked about this whole Jeep chase thing. Or the reason we're on an island that holds some bullshit treasure and a submarine full of God knows what." Skyler told him.

Daxton reached into the cooler and pulled out two Pacificos.

He popped the top and handed one to Skyler opened his and took a big slug "Do you remember Parks from when you were younger?"

"No" Skyler answered. "But I watch his show where he never finds anything now. I knew you guys were friends."

"There is something here. Parks just didn't get a chance to find it. After all of this, I say we spend some time digging into it." Daxton told her.

"Dad, Parks is a treasure hunter and a face that people want to see. He found two treasures and now he has a spot on

Discovery. If he wanted it bad enough, he would have drug it out of here."

"Probably so baby girl, probably so."

Daxton put the boat on course and headed back to the harbor. The lighting was perfect over Palm Island, and he looked over his shoulders and slowly headed out. The palms slowly swayed, and the seas swelled. As Daxton watched the island disappear, he couldn't help but think about what was on that sub and also what the treasure could be that Parks never uncovered. But now his thoughts were taken over by the fact that his daughter, Kelsey, and all the others needed him more than ever. "Put a pin in it Dax" he said to himself as they headed toward the mainland.

CHAPTER TWENTY TWO

The sport fisher slowly came to a halt just a couple hundred yards off the shoreline of Palm Island. Everyone on the boat could hear the boat throttle down and they knew they were closing in to the site. Liam tried to help Skyler as she pulled the scuba tank from the side of the boat cabinet. "I got it Liam, but thanks," she said as she grabbed the tank and threw it onto her shoulder, and headed for the back of the boat.

Daxton cleared the aircraft lines on his setup and shot a few blasts into the air. "Heya Sky, when you get yours all locked and loaded let's double check the communication gear."

"Okay give me just a few Dad. Did we confirm that the sub is sitting around eighty feet deep?"

Mateo peeked his head out of the cabin of the Sport Fisher. "The depth indicator shows eighty-two feet and it's sitting on a nice flat rock for you. I can still see all the surroundings through the side scan radar. The batteries only fire when I shoot signals to the submarine. They aren't enough any longer to provide the thrust and ballast we need to get to the drop zone. I can assure you Ms. Shaw it's sitting at eighty-two feet deep."

Skyler looked at Mateo. "You sure seem very smart to be mixed up with this kind of thing. I completely believe you so that's what we will aim for." Daxton adjusted his BC as Kelsey walked up to him. "I'm going to tell you this again Dax, you take care of our little girl down there. I'm not sure what we're getting into, but you take care of her!"

Daxton stood up and grabbed Kelsey by the hand. He said, "Look Kels, I lost you already a long time ago and I'm not about to lose her! Ever!"

Liam watched in silence from the top deck as Daxton and Kelsey stared into each other's eyes for just a little too long. He wasn't upset or jealous. He knew that they were still in love with each other. He had heard her cry herself to sleep on many nights.

"You have my word as always Kelsey." He dropped her hand and looked up at Liam. He could see that Liam knew there was still something between him and Kelsey. Their gaze was broken when Skyler tossed him a dive knife.

"We have ten minutes to be on the water Dad. You need to get your gear rolling." Daxton rolled his eyes at Kelsey and headed to the back of the deck. "Alright, kiddo, what's the plan?" Skyler handed Daxton a small screwdriver with a custom-patterned tip.

"Mateo says that this is the only type of tool that can open the hatch on the cargo hold to remove the case." The tool had a small cinch leash that Daxton slid up his arm and cinched tight. He told Skyler, "I'll take care of getting the hatch open. Once we get the case removed you connect the lines, inflate the lift bag, and get the case to the surface like we talked about."

Deal, check, check one two, one two. Kelsey's voice could be heard coming from a small communication box. They all checked their communication systems a few times and started to suit up in their gear.

Liam looked back out over the top of the boat. "Is there anything you need me to do Mr. Shaw?"

Daxton looked at Skyler and she shook her head no.

"We're all good here Liam. Just make sure the anchor holds and you're here when we come back up. Depending on how the hatch cooperates we honestly shouldn't be more than forty minutes or so. When you see the inflation bag pop up that means we aren't too far behind."

Daxton and Skyler backed up and sat down on the edge of the Sport Fisher. He reached over and grabbed Skyler on the knee. "You have no idea how proud of you I am Sky. And it's so great to get some bottom time with you again. I love you more than you can imagine kiddo."

Skyler fought back her emotions. "I love you too Dad. Quit your crying. It will just fog up your mask!"

Daxton laughed and they both slid their masks over their faces. Skyler gave the thumbs up, and they simultaneously rolled backward into the warm ocean waters off the shoreline of Palm Island.

Daxton and Skyler hit the crystal-clear blue waters back first.

Once they were underwater, they repositioned themselves and did one more quick gear check.

"You sure you still remember how to do this Dad? I mean unless there's a bar underwater, I don't see you diving much."

"That's a low blow, Sky but a damn good idea. Maybe if we get this behind us we can open one underwater." The comment hurt but in Daxton fashion he turned it into something to laugh about.

"Only if you guys let me drop out of college."

Kelsey raced over to the microphone and keyed it saying to Skyler, "Not happening Sky!" Skyler ignored her and started to dump air from her buoyancy compensator. As she and Daxton slowly descended into the depths they began surveying the layout. The light began to dim and as they fell the submarine came into view. "Wow, that's cool as shit!" Skyler said, From the microphone up top came a "Mouth, Sky, mouth!" Daxton was about to say the same thing before Kelsey beat him to it.

The submarine was a beautiful work of art. Slender, the dark blue panels glistened as the sun rays danced across the topside.

Skyler and Daxton made a lap around the sub for a quick inspection. "Heya, Liam, you sure got a nice toy down here. She's sitting on her belly and doesn't appear to have any damage."

Mateo got on the microphone. "It's not a toy and I told you it would be fine."

Daxton said, "Easy Mateo, it's not a toy. Just givin' Liam a hard time." He slowly settled down to the roof of the submarine. "Okay Mateo, I see the forward hatch. Anything special we didn't go over?"

"No, once you open the hatch the container area will flood so if you get anything you will get a large air bubble that releases. The sub will not flood. Just that compartment." Mateo replied.

"Ten-four Mateo. About to start getting her opened" Daxton ran his hand across the screws and slowly ran the tool on the lanyard down onto his wrist.

"Don't drop that tool, Dad. It looks like an extremely long way down that ledge." Daxton looked over the sub and down into the abyss telling Skyler, Yeah, she's a deep one over there Sky." He started unscrewing the first screw. It backed out slowly but nicely and evenly. Then the second and on until the sixth.

Skyler started pulling out the lift bag and getting all the lines untangled. "Okay Dad, the lift bag is ready to go," she said. One more screw Daxton told her as he slowly turned the last screw. The hatch was still solid, so he pulled out his dive knife and pried the lid open.

The giant air bubble pushed the lid open and erupted into the water passing over Daxton. As the water settled Daxton and Skyler both swam in closer to the payload. Daxton reached in and unclipped the top rack and the black case was loose. He slid it out and laid it on the roof of the submarine telling Skyler "Okay, Sky. Let's get her up to the surface."

As Skyler started to inflate the lift bag, they were surprised to hear the noise of a propeller moving closer. Daxton immediately contacted their boat. "Hey guys, what's going on up there? We hear a boat coming in."

Liam ran down the deck and grabbed the mic. "We have company, Mr. Shaw. Stay put for the time being".

Skyler looked at Daxton asking, "Are we okay, Dad?" Daxton replied, "I don't know Sky, let's just sit down here and stay off the coms for a bit until we hear back. How's your air Sky?"

Skyler told him," I'm good for fifteen minutes or so. I will slow it down a little if I can."

Daxton gave her the thumbs up and looked up at the boat that slowed and made its way to their sport fisher.

"Good morning, can I help you gentlemen with something? Are we in restricted waters or something?" He chuckled a bit playing into his own act. Four men stood on the boat looking at Liam, all very callous and expressionless. Mark walked to the edge of the boat and pulled a pistol from out of the back of his pants waistband. He stuck it in Liam's face and looked directly into his eyes.

"No, these are not restricted waters and yes, you can absolutely help me with something. I need you to call down to your divers and let them know someone is here to pick up that case."

"We don't have any way to communicate with them", Liam said.

Mark wasn't in the mood to play Liam's game and said, "I can promise you this Liam. Neither you, Mateo, Daxton, Kelsey, Scott, or Skyler want to fuck with me! Reach over there now and get on your little intercom system and you tell your divers that someone is here to pick up that package! If you don't comply, I will kill all of you and go down and get it myself. It's really that easy." Mark's voice was elevated and menacing as he got closer to Liam's face with the Springfield 1911.

Kelsey yelled at Liam "Call down to them now Liam! Just give him what he wants! Please!" Liam took a deep breath, knowing he would put his life on the line for the contents of the case. But not yet. He felt he had time to get control of the situation. He picked up the mic and squeezed the button on the side. "Hey guys, go ahead and send up the case. Someone is here to pick it up. We're all good up here."

Daxton looked over at Skyler. He pointed to her communication system on her mask. He motioned to switch it to where the topside could not hear their conversation. They both turned the setting and started quickly talking at the same time. Daxton put his hand up motioning to Skyler to quit talking. "This does not feel right at all Skyler. I have no idea what is going on up there, but I promise you It's not good."

Skyler asked, "So what the hell do we do"

"Your Mom is up there. We stick to the plan until we get a visual of what's going on. We can't risk it. We have to send it up."

Skyler shook her head, yes, quickly agreeing. "Okay, okay Skyler said as she started taking deeper breaths. Daxton swam over to her and looked at her mask to mask.

"Baby, we are going to be okay. Whatever is going on up there we will handle it. Now I need you to breathe and relax. We got this, together."

Skyler consciously worked to calm her breathing and pulled the lift bag out from under her arm.

"That's my girl," Daxton told her in a reassuring way. He pulled the clips apart and connected them all to the case. He flipped on his topside setting on his computer system. "Sorry about that Liam. I had it in the wrong setting. Loud and clear and about to send the payload up. Should be breaking the surface in a few minutes just off the starboard side of the boat." Daxton grabbed Skyler by her BC vest and looked into her scared eyes while telling her "Look, I need you to stay strong and follow my lead if need be. I love you Sky with all that's in me. We got this girl."

A tear ran down Skyler's cheek and she took a deep breath. She knew her Dad wasn't scared of anything, but she was. "I love you too Dad."

Daxton tapped Skyler playfully on the side of her head and winked. "Alright, kiddo, let's get up there and say hello to our guests.

CHAPTER TWENTY THREE

The lift bag quickly broke the surface of the calm waters as the case dangled a few feet below. Mark pointed the gun at Liam and Scott then back at Mateo who stood on the back of the deck.

"Kelsey is going to accompany me on our vessel until we have retrieval of the case and it's in our possession. Now, come over here sweetheart, and let's go get the case. Your ex-husband and daughter should be back here real soon."

Liam yelled at Mark. "No deal, no fuckling deal! She stays here!" Mark aimed his pistol at the flybridge and shot a hole in the top of the fiberglass.

" Stop! Stop it, I will go Liam. It's okay. Just do what he says!" Kelsey screamed and made her way over to the boat Mark was in. Liam watched as Mark grabbed her hand to help her make her way into his boat. His blood began to boil but he knew Kelsey was right, at least in that current state. Scott looked up at Liam and Liam shook his head not sensing what Scott wanted to do.

"Now that is a smart woman right there see. Sensible and beautiful. We will all be on our way and never see each other again in just a few short minutes. Don't do anything foolish and again, we will all go on about our way."

As Kelsey boarded the boat Mark motioned for one of his men to start the boat and head toward the lift bag. The boat engines sprang to life, and they slowly made their way to the payload.

Skyler slowly took the lead and started toward the surface a little quicker than Daxton. Daxton grabbed her by the ankle and pulled her back. She looked back and glared at him. He shook his head no and made a hand movement telling her to slow down. Skyler's breathing rate was up, and she could almost hear her heartbeat in her mask. He tapped her again and pointed to the boat making its way to the lift bag that rested on the surface. Skyler acknowledged and tried to regain her composure.

Liam's cell phone rested on the console. He briefly looked down not to cause alarm as he heard it vibrate. He had sent a test message as he watched the boat approach asking for help. The message that came back simply said, "On our way!"

Liam reached under the console and slowly felt the outline of his pistol as one of the men in Mark's boat yelled and pointed at the water. Liam pulled his hand back up and walked to the edge of the boat.

"There they are, they're coming up!". Mark looked back at his guy yelling and pointing at the water. "C'mon, man. Let's not get all excited and scare everyone. It's just the stars of the show today on a happy swim!"

Daxton pulled Skyler back down and slowly made his way between her and the boat that was slowly backing up toward them. He looked at her one more time, winked, and made the okay symbol with his hand. Skyler quickly shook her head yes and signaled the okay sign back. As the water surface grew closer and closer, Daxton could see Kelsey standing on the back of the boat with someone he didn't know behind her. He calmed his breathing as he and Skyler slowly breached the surface of the water.

"Good morning, guys. I gotta ask first, how was your dive experience today?". Daxton could see the pistol in the stranger's right hand. He could also see the other men standing in the background with H&K MP5s slung across their chests. He knew he needed to play this one calm and collected just as he also knew these guys were trained and not the typical pirates he had seen in the past. He slowly pulled the full-face mask from his head.

"You know, I've never really been a fan of diving around Mexico, but today completely changed my mind. There are some interesting things to see down there. I mean, things I've never seen in my lifetime." Skyler took off her mask and could also see the man with the gun standing next to her mother and the other men behind her. She kept her calm as her Dad slowly paddled his way toward the boat.

"You good Kels? Daxton questioned. She shook her head yes in silence. "So, I'm no detective but I'm going to go out on a limb here and say you guys want whatever is in that case over there."

Mark threw his hand in the air. "Well hallelujah! There are two of you who just know how to get to business. Look, I know it's none of my business, but you guys should have just stayed married. I mean, look at you two. Match made in heaven. And look at that gorgeous daughter you have." Daxton's facial expression instantly changed when Mark mentioned Skyler and Mark could tell.

"No, no, no! No harm or disrespect to you, Mr. Shaw. You guys should be proud parents. She is so versed in the world already at such a young age. Anyway, moving on from the bullshit, yes, that's why we're here. We want the case. We want nothing else. You put the case into this boat, Kelsey gets back on your boat and we both cruise off into the sunset."

Daxton looked up at Liam, Scott, and Mateo. "You guys all good over there?" he yelled. They all gave the thumbs-up sign except for Scott who yelled back, "All good over here boss! Are you good? "Daxon and Skyler both threw the okay hand signal.

"Alright, Sky let's wrangle that bag and get it over to our company.

Liam watched closely as they swam toward the lift bag. Mark looked back up at Liam and then back at Daxton and Skyler. As they made their way closer to the bag Skyler whispered to Daxton. "What's the plan? What are we doing Dad?" "Absolutely nothing Sky, we are outgunned, outmanned, and outboated. We give them the case and see how it goes from there. We stand zero chance of success if we make a move here but whatever happens, do not get on that boat!" Daxton wrapped the cords up around his arm, turned around, and started swimming back toward the boat. "Do you hear me Sky?" Daxton repeated. "Yes, I hear you and I promise I won't."

The two of them paddled their way closer to the back of Mark's boat. As Daxton got somewhat closer to the boat Mark's face loomed before him. He remembered Mark's face! That guy's been trailing us around town for weeks he thought as he wrangled the case up into his hand.

"Okay, can you guys drop that swim platform for me? I'll throw the case up there then you let her get back on our boat. How's that sound?"

"A deal is a deal, Mr. Shaw," Mark told him. He motioned to his men to pull the lines taught back into the sport fisher. As the boats got closer and closer Liam was losing his nerve. His greed and determination to succeed took over his rational thinking concerning the situation.

The men dropped the platform into the water and Daxton proceeded to throw the case up onto the deck. Mark's face lit up as he stared at the case laid out in front of him. Daxton was not very close to Mark as he leaned over to inspect the case. Mark was saying, "Okay bud, let's let her go, no reason to let this….

Shots rang out and bullets pierced the hull of Mark's boat. Two rounds hit the water just feet from where Daxton and Kelsey trod water. Mark grabbed the case and took cover lying in the back of the boat. Kelsey also got down to deck level as Liam reached for another clip. "My whole fucking life and career is in that case! It's mine and you aren't taking it!" He jammed another clip into the bottom of the pistol.

Scott watched Mark's guards pull their weapons into place. He ran across the deck grabbing hold of Mateo as he did. They both cleared the side of the boat. As Scott and Mateo hit the water the guards opened fire on the Sport Fisher throwing Fiberglass, wood, and pieces of the boat into the air.

Liam continued to squeeze the trigger aiming at their boat until he took one round to the abdomen, and another grazed his neck. It sent him to the deck instantly.

The bullets slowed as Mark yelled. "Go! go! go!"

One of the men leaped in to help and slammed the throttle forward as Daxton yelled, "Jump Kelsey, jump!" But as Kelsey ran to jump Mark grabbed her and threw her forcefully toward the back of the boat. He aimed the pistol at Daxton and Skyler and began firing. "Dive Sky! Now!! They both took a deep breath and as they went down a bullet hit the top of Skyler's tank. It didn't penetrate the tank, but it rang so loud it almost knocked her unconscious. They held their breath for about thirty seconds before they broke the surface only to see Mark's boat getting more and more distance between them. Before they could process or even think, they could hear Liam yelling "Go to the island! More help is coming. Go now!" Daxton could see that Liam wasn't in good shape, blood dripped from his mouth as he yelled.

"Liam, No! We have to get Kelsey back!" Daxton screamed.

He could see Scott and Mateo swimming around the side of the Sport Fisher.

"That's what I'm doing Mr. Shaw. Her and the case!" Mark hammered the throttle, and the rear of the boat sank low while exhaust billowed from the engine housing. As the boat peeled off in pursuit Skyler began to cry. Daxton slammed his hand on the water and cussed profusely. Scott and Mateo swam over to them and calmed them down knowing they had to begin swimming their way over to Palm Island.

CHAPTER TWENTY FOUR

Liam pushed the throttle as far forward as he could. He slipped in his own blood when the boat accelerated even more. He could feel himself getting weak and cold and knew he was not doing well. He reached down and stuck his finger close to his abdomen wound. "Ahhhh, Fuck!" he screamed in pain as he punched the center console. He wiped the blood from his mouth with his sleeve and focused his attention on the boat speeding away in front of him. He picked up his cell phone and called his reinforcement team. "You're going to see two boats headed north.

One is me. Do not stop! Get to the divers and my two crew who will be swimming to or already on Palm Island!"

"Now what the hell do we do Dad? They have Mom!" Skyler looked at her father as she swam backward with tears in her eyes.

"Liam said more help is coming. We wait. I cannot believe that son of a bitch left us! He couldn't fight his way out of a paper sack and besides that, he probably has about an hour left to live."

"Dad, what is wrong with you!" Skyler shrieked. Scott chimed in, "I'm sorry Skyler but your Dad is right. The rounds he took and the blood he was losing didn't give him much time."

Daxton looked Mateo in the eyes with a death stare and grabbed him by the shirt while they bobbed in the water.

"What the fuck is in that case? Tell me now what's in there Mateo! What are we dealing with that's so fucking important?"

Daxton yelled in his face, but Mateo was quiet. "What's in the goddamn case Mateo?" Scott swam over and drug Daxton off Mateo. "Calm down boss. We're all shook up. We will get your wife back. Daxton pulled away from Scott and swam faster away, toward the shoreline of the island.

Just as Liam thought he was losing ground to catch up with the speeding boat it seemed he was closing the gap. He squinted at the boat before grabbing the binoculars off the dash. He pulled them up to his face and it looked as if the boat had stopped in the water. What are you doing asshole, he spoke aloud to himself. He made his way down to the quarters leaving a blood trail down the ladder and along the floor. He opened the cabin door and made his way to the couch. He pulled the cushion off and a false wooden bottom out of the couch and unstrapped the AR-15 that was mounted to the floor. He pulled the slide and racked a round into the chamber. With difficulty, he slung the rifle over his shoulder and proceeded to make his way back up to the flybridge. His hand slipped on the bloody rung, and it took everything in him to make his way back up. He unslung the rifle and put it on the dash as he was closing in on Mark's vessel. At the same time, he was watching the backup team off in the distance head toward Palm Island, but his focus turned back to the boat he had in his sights.

As he got closer, he could see Kelsey screaming as Mark pushed her to the deck and pointed his pistol at her. He could also see a helicopter off in the distance closing in on Mark's boat.

Liam grabbed the AR-15 up to his shoulder and pulled the trigger. He fired a quick ten rounds at the boat, aiming high so he didn't hit Kelsey yelling "Remember me mother fucker?" Liam yelled as Mark's henchmen moved to the back of the boat and opened fire on him. Fiberglass pieces flew everywhere, and Liam ducked his head screaming "Hahahaha, you missed this time!" He pulled his rifle back up and emptied the remaining twenty rounds in return fire hitting one of the men in the throat.

Blood squirted from his neck all over Kelsey and Mark. Kelsey could tell Mark was distracted as he turned his attention to Liam's boat and started to fire his pistol at it.

The helicopter was now hovering almost over Mark's boat and Kelsey made her way to the edge of the boat and jumped over. Mark turned and frantically searched for her in the water until he saw her. He fired rounds into the water at Kelsey and one round grazed her thigh spilling her blood into the water. Bullets were hitting all around Liam and he painfully ran to the front of the boat no longer worried about Kelsey. Two men on the back of

Mark's boat started to reload their rifles with drum clips at the same time Liam was slamming a new thirty-round clip into the bottom of the AR. Liam was sweating, feeling light-headed and in pain as he pulled his weapon up to his shoulder.

He pulled the trigger as fast as he could hitting both men, but Liam's bullets didn't take them down immediately and they took aim at the boat and Liam letting the fully automatic MP5s open fire. Round after round sprayed the boat and more than five rounds hit Liam in the chest and torso. He hit the deck hard. The boat started smoking and a small fire started in the front of the boat where the generator had been hit.

At the same time, the helicopter lowered and dropped a rope ladder down to the deck of Mark's boat. One of his men lay dying on the back deck. Mark approached him, shot him point blank and his body went limp as he took his final breath. Feeling no remorse, Mark reached into his pocket pulled out a small tube, and banged it on the side of the boat. The tube burst into a hot phosphorescent flame, and he threw it to the back of the boat next to the engine hatch, grabbed the case, and reached out for the ladder. The ladder slowly began to rise, and Mark rode it up until he was at the helicopter. He threw the case in and jumped into the chopper. He surveyed what looked like a war zone below and watched as both boats had smoke pouring from them.

Kelsey knew she was hit but she didn't know the extent of the wound. As she swam toward the sport fisher the burning tube melted through the fiberglass and dropped into the engine housing. The fumes were ignited and instantly it was engulfed in flames. She could feel the heat coming from the boat and heard the helicopter getting further away.

Although she knew she wasn't out of the woods she felt better knowing it was leaving. She swam up to the sport fisher and she could see Liam lying on the flybridge not moving as she climbed the ladder. She hurried, yelling his name as she made her way to him. Kelsey lay down next to Liam. She picked up his head and started crying.

"Liam, no, please no! Wake up!" She checked his pulse, and it was weak. She noticed the massive amount of blood. She saw the holes in his body and knew there was no way she could help him. Liam choked on his own blood and fluttered his eyes as Kelsey held his head. "Kelsey, please have a great life. Thank you for being with me.", he whispered weakly.

Kelsey screamed at him "Don't let go, Liam, don't do it!" Liam closed his eyes and took one last deep breath. He murmured slowly, "Go to…. your family." His body went limp as Kelsey held him. She sobbed and kissed his forehead. She sat for a minute and collected her thoughts. She could tell the flames were growing and getting louder. She reached up and unclasped the necklace from her neck and placed it around Liam's neck. "I never deserved this from you Liam," she whispered. "Go in peace and thank you for loving me and my daughter."

She knew she had to go and there was no time left to spare. She stood up to make her way off the boat when it exploded sending fiberglass, wood, and metal through the air and into the water.

Daxton, Skyler, Scott, and Mateo watched as the boat exploded into thousands of pieces as the gigantic black cloud rolled on itself over the ocean waters.

CHAPTER TWENTY FIVE

The boat went silent as they watched the mushroom cloud elevate higher into the air.

"Dad! Skyler came out of the fog they were all in and ran over to Daxton. "Mom! Mom was on that boat!"

Daxton yelled at the captain. "Get us over there now!" The captain yelled back at him.

"We aren't getting any closer than this for now. We don't know what else was on that boat!"

Daxton charged the helm, grabbed the captain, and threw him back onto the deck. "The hell we aren't!" he exclaimed as he threw it into full power and headed toward the burning chaos. He yelled over the noise of the speeding boat, "Skyler, look for anyone in the water now!" Skyler ran over to the edge of the boat and started frantically scanning the water surface in the area. As Daxton got closer, they could see the water littered with debris. The flames danced on the water's surface as the fuel made its way up from the half-sunken ships. "Dad! Dad! Over there. It's Mom! Skyler yelled. There she is!"

Daxton looked over the port side and could see Kelsey floating on her back in the water.

Daxton said nothing as he ran and dove off the boat.

Scott was only a few seconds behind him also diving into the water. Both swam at Olympic time to get to Kelsey. Once they reached her Daxton checked for a pulse and kissed her face. He felt nothing. "Dammit, Kels, c'mon, not like this. C'mon!" He swam underneath her and put his arms under her shoulders. "She's not breathing Scott; she's not fucking breathing!"

Scott swam closer and put his ear to her mouth. He reached his fingers up on her neck and checked for a pulse. He looked at Daxton telling him, "We have to get her back boss. Hold her tight, tell her you love her." Scott moved into position and started CPR the best he could in the water. "Tell her boss!" Scott did chest compressions with Daxton holding onto her back and then blew into her mouth as Daxton whispered in her ear. "Kels, come back to me and things will be different. I love you so damn much and I miss you. You have to come back to me so we can fix it together. I'll make it up to you, I swear! Without you we have nothing. Please, baby, come back. Please!" Daxton started crying and held her head as Scott proceeded to work on her. Daxton took a deep breath and changed his tone. "Kelsey Michelle Shaw!!, you are not fucking done yet! You're just getting started. Don't be selfish!! You have Skyler and me and we need you! We need you!

Stop playing around and…" Scott pressed on her chest one last time and Kelsey spat out what looked like a gallon of water. She took a gigantic breath of air and choked for a few seconds. "Kelsey, I'm here baby and I'm never leaving you. Never again. I'm so sorry baby, I'm so sorry!"

Kelsey choked on more water and coughed, then she felt a calm come over her body. As she came fully around, she found herself floating face up in the ocean in Daxton's embrace. "You promise me that Daxton Shaw?"

Daxton's lower lip quivered, and tears ran down his face. He turned her to him and kissed her gently. "I meant every word of it Kels."

Skyler watched silently from the boat with tears running down her cheeks.

"C'mon, boss. Let's get her to the boat." Mateo swam over to assist and the four of them made their way back to the boat. "Skyler, can you see anyone else? We need to find Liam." Daxton told her. Kelsey pursed her lips and shook her head. "He didn't make it Daxton, there's no one else alive. Daxton turned his head and watched the last of the boat hull sink into the blue water saying, "I'm sorry Kelsey." And he meant it.

Scott and Daxton swam next to the boat and Skyler reached down to grab Kelsey's hand as the tears poured down her face. She could barely put together a sentence. "I thought you were gone, Mom." As Kelsey cleared the edge of the boat, she pulled Skyler in for a huge hug and held onto her as tightly as she could.

"I'm here Sky. I'm here forever baby. I love you and I'm so sorry for all this. It's all my fault" She pushed Skyler back so she could look at her and she reached up and slowly wiped the tears away from her face. "It's okay baby, we are all okay." Skyler noticed that Kelsey's necklace was missing, and she ran her hand over her mother's neck where the necklace had lain. It went back to its rightful owner and was the only thing Kelsey could sadly tell Skyler.

Scott jumped into the boat and started helping Mateo and Daxton back in. Kelsey was beginning to feel somewhat normal despite feeling extremely exhausted from her ordeal. She made her way slowly to Daxton and the others as they were climbing aboard. Daxton hugged her again.

"What happened out there, Kelsey?" He hated to ask her now, but he needed to know.

"Mark and those other guys shot up Liam's boat and killed Liam. By the time I made it to Liam, well, he died shortly after I reached him." "What about the other boat?' Daxton asked.

"Liam returned fire and I think he hit them a couple of times. A helicopter flew in and picked up Mark but not before he killed his own men on that boat."

"So, a helicopter came and got Mark. And the case?"

Kelsey said yes, he had the case with him.

Daxton turned to Mateo. "We have a pretty good boat ride to get to a safe place until things settle out. I need to make sure all of this is off the radar. It won't take long to find out if anyone will come looking for us or the boats. You are going to tell us everything about what's going on and what's in that case. Do you understand?" Mateo shook his head yes.

Daxton hugged Skyler and kissed Kelsey on the forehead. He asked Kelsey if she was okay to travel before telling everyone to get a seat. "We have to get out of here now."

Daxton got to the helm, he made sure everyone was seated before he hammered the throttles forward. As the boat left the scene everyone's eyes fixated on the debris field and the flames that continued to burn on the water's surface.

CHAPTER TWENTY SIX

Daxton cleared his salty brown hair from his eyes and looked over the horizon and then toward the back of the boat. Everyone aboard was quiet, and Skyler was lying across Kelsey's lap. Kelsey looked toward Daxton and caught his sideways grin that she had always loved. Daxton motioned for one of the men to take the helm, instructing him to stay on the course set and maintain the same speed. Then he made his way to the back of the boat and knelt next to Skyler. "It's okay baby, I know this has been a lot for you Sky, but we are going to be okay. I promise you. And I also promise you that things will be different." He stood up and got his footing when Mateo walked up to them. Mateo took a deep breath and said, "I want you all to know the truth and I will tell you but once I tell you these things it could possibly change your lives." Daxton, Kelsey, and Skyler gave Mateo the go-ahead after they decided they all wanted to know. Mateo sat down in the seat next to them. He rested his face in his hands for a moment and then looked up.

"Have any of you ever heard of the Amber Room?" They looked at each other and Skyler sat up from her mother's lap. "It was a room built from amber, gold, and jewels. I think it was built in the 1700s in Prussia. I'm pretty sure I fell asleep in that class a lot but I want to say it was blown up."

Mateo pointed at Skyler. "That's partially correct and there was a lot of speculation about what happened to the Amber Room but in short, it was not blown up. In 1941 the Nazis were looting artifacts; art, gold, jewels, and anything that held historic value all over the territories they had infiltrated and eventually occupied. The Amber Room was on Hitler's most wanted list, and he retrieved it. It was disassembled and pieces of it were hung in one of the bunkers he spent the most time in."

Scott looked at Mateo. "So, all of this is over some panels from the Amber Room that hung in Hitler's bunker? I had Cindy Crawford posters in my room." he joked. "Seriously though, all of this for just some panels of that room?"

Mateo shook his head no. "It's not about the panels. It's about what was on the panels. There was a weapon that was constructed. A weapon that could change the world as we know it. A weapon that could have ended most of the life on Earth. This weapon was called the Zerstorer, this is translated in English to "Destroyer". They had many tests with the weapon, and it was ninety-nine percent ready when the regimen fell. While Hitler was in isolation, he stamped codes on the back of these panels that would help redesign the Zerstorer but the only problem was that the main designs were in one of his many journals. The code is worthless without the journal."

Daxton looked curiously at Mateo. "So, what good are the panels if they don't have the journal?"

"Well, Mr. Shaw, that's the thing. The panels along with Hitler's journal were in that case." Everyone was processing the information that Mateo was feeding them. Daxton stood up. "So, you're telling me that in eighty years these things have been missing and no government has been involved in finding the plans for this weapon of mass destruction?"

"Yes, Mr. Shaw, they have. These items were located at the bottom of a lake almost ten years ago by a private treasure hunter and before the government could track down its location it disappeared once again." Mateo answered.

Daxton addressed Mateo, "So when we get to shore, we need to alert the correct people to let them know it has been found again. Obviously, whoever that guy was, he was not the right person to possess it. We call someone and we are done with this whole thing!"

"I really wish it was that easy Mr. Shaw but we are now accomplices in the theft of the items. We will be tried and punished to the maximum extent possible. I don't think...."

Daxton interjected mid-sentence. Then you're telling me we all just have to go into hiding for the remainder of our lives? Or do we have to track that guy who obviously has an endless amount of backing and gun power? Sounds freaking awesome. I don't know about the rest of you but I'm so glad Liam decided to get us all involved in his shit show. I mean Nazis, weapons of mass destruction, theft of a priceless artifact, four people dead, and two boats at the bottom of the ocean now. Daxton shook his head, turned, and stared over the ocean lost in his own thoughts.

"To be fair Mr. Shaw, we all chose to be here. I'm not even sure my family is alive. Mark said he would kill my family if the plan failed. The plan failed. But there is another option. I made some plans of my own along the way."

Daxton turned back to face Mateo. "Tell me about this other option Mateo."

Mateo responded, "He does not have the real panels."

"I'm not following you Mateo. He doesn't have the real panels?" questioned Daxton.

"Mr. Shaw, he does not. As you can see the sun is resting on a perfect ledge. It's within distance of the Palm Island shoreline. I placed the sub in that location. As it sat and we waited for the local military to leave, I had the panels switched. I had four panels recreated that were flawless. The codes on the back of the panels will make no sense to anyone. As for the journal, he does possess the real one at this point but again, it's worthless without the codes.

"Jesus, Mateo! Did you steal from a guy like that? What's your move now? Where are the panels?" Daxton was impressed and irritated at the same time.

Mateo stood up, circled around, and pointed to Palm Island.

"They are on the island Mr. Shaw. They will be safe until we go back and retrieve them."

CHAPTER TWENTY SEVEN

It was January 7, 1944 in Landsberg, Germany in a large, unmarked brick building sat along a snowy hillside. Large German semi-trucks moved in and out of the heavily guarded metal gates. Adolph Hitler and Himmler pulled up in their caravan of four vehicles. The gate arm lifted, and they were immediately waved through toward the compounds. The Nazi flags on the front of the limo fluttered in the freezing air as they sped up to the building. A large door in the front of the building slowly opened and the caravan pulled inside. Men hurried around the side of the cars and opened the doors for Hitler and Himmler. Hitler carried a leather-bound book and a small briefcase. The men saluted them as they walked through the building and into an extremely large sterile room. There in the center of the room sat a very large smooth metallic object.

There were large half rings that extended outward from the center hexagon; the rings had what appeared to be nozzles pointing back toward the center of the contraption. In the center of the device, the hexagon gave off a green mirror-like appearance. The reflections of the scientists bounced around as they worked closely with the unit. As Hitler walked around the object scientists scurried around the room and began to move the ladders and man lifts back away from the object.

Hitler walked up and ran his gloved hand across one of the arms. "I want to see the machine operate." He spoke in a very firm tone.

"We are still working on a few last items Fuhrer, it should be ready in a couple of days," responded the lead scientist.

"No! I want to see it operate now. I was told it would be operational by now!" yelled Hitler.

The scientist knew better than to question Hitler, so he made a few hand gestures to the other scientists in the room. He walked up and closed a small panel on the device and connected a large four-inch diameter cord to the underside of the machine. All the other personnel in the room began moving to the viewing shelter. Hitler walked in last and stood directly in front of the glass, his hands were behind him, and he peered at the device. Hirsch made his way into the room and started making adjustments to the control panels.

"Okay, gentlemen, this will be test number seven. We will bring the device online for no longer than fifteen seconds during this testing phase. At that time, we will shut down the device and start our post-operational evaluations. No one is to enter the room until we have checked for signs of extreme radiation."

The scientists nodded their understanding, conforming to the commands. They were lined up behind Hitler looking through the thick protective glass. Hirsch placed his hand on a steel handle and slowly moved it forward. The center of the machine slowly started to spin in a counterclockwise direction. The room was silent as Hirsch pushed the level up a little further. The rings were now spinning at a high rate of speed. Hirsch reached down and flipped a small red cover off of the lighted switch with his thumb.

The level indicator was at the lowest mark of the gauge when he flipped the illuminated switch into the ON position. Particles flowed out of the nozzles and into the center of the mirrorlike surface. A huge cracking sound shook the building as a large green ball appeared within the center of the device. The rings were spinning a glow that was almost blinding. The onlookers could barely look through the window due to its overwhelming brilliance. Hitler smiled, knowing they had harnessed the power needed to run his new super weapons. He motioned to increase the power and Hirsch hesitated for a brief Moment. Hitler insisted once again, and Hirsch pushed the handle one notch higher. The device began spinning even faster and a piercing sound came over the entire area. A massive green beam shot from the device into the ceiling. Everyone in the room quickly put their hand to their ears in an effort to muffle the piercing sound. The protective glass surrounding the viewing area exploded into thousands of pieces and rained down on everyone in the room. Hirsch jumped up while shielding his face from the debris, he hit the emergency stop button and the machine slowly began to wind down. The luminescence of the green ball of light slowly diminished as the machine slowed down and stopped spinning.

The scientists started picking themselves up from the ground as Hitler stood up quickly before his bodyguards could reach him.

"Good work gentlemen! I will expect to see it powering the Zestorer in two weeks. I want to do a field test of the weapon in four days."

They were all amazed to see the calmness of the Fuhrer after what had just taken place. He brushed the glass from his jacket and walked out of the room.

His guards followed closely behind him and loaded him into his limo.

Hirsch approached another of the head scientists and looked at him directly in the eyes "We have created something that could change the course of mankind; I hope we have done the right thing." He turned and headed back to the machine in disbelief and fear of the thing they had created

CHAPTER TWENTY EIGHT

As the sun began to set over the ocean ripples the boat slowed as it crept into the dilapidated makeshift harbor. Kelsey looked around and then over at Skyler. They both shrugged but they knew Daxton obviously had a plan. "Will they be greeting us on the dock with a cocktail and take our bags Dax?" she quipped. She was trying to mask the mental and physical pain by trying to lighten the mood. The boat ride had been relatively quiet after Mateo explained what was going on.

Daxton looked to one of Liam's men, "Look guys, you'll never understand how grateful we all are. You gentlemen could have left us out there. You could have turned and run but you didn't and more than likely you have saved all our lives. We are truly grateful for what Liam provided. He appeared to be somewhat of a good man, though misguided in some ways. Once we get to shore, I'll give you a map and directions on how to get out of here. You can follow the shoreline and it won't take you long to get back where you came from. We will speak no more about what happened today and I'm sure you will do the same." The man looked at Daxton and stuck his hand out for a shake. He firmly shook Daxton's hand saying, "You are welcome. Liam would have wanted it that way. All of this never happened, and it will not be discussed on our end."

Daxton replied, "Thank you again. My family and my friend here thank you as well." He motioned toward Kelsey, Skyler, and Scott.

The boat slowly motored close to a pier that had about every four deck planks left standing. Scott jumped on the bow and grabbed the lines as Daxton threw it in reverse and slid the boat sideways as close to the rickety docks as possible. Mateo handled the aft lines and both men tied the boat off to the pylons. Scott jumped off first to help everyone else off the boat one by one. They each carefully maneuvered to the land at the end of the broken-down pier.

"If I didn't have Hep C before this will surely do the trick," Skyler said as she followed her Dad's movements down the pier.

Once they made it to dry land they briefly rested before surveying the area.

Daxton approached a man who was burning trash in a fifty-gallon steel drum and began speaking Spanish to him while Kelsey talked to Liam's crewmen. "Please tell Liam's family that he was a good man. He was passionate and died chasing what he wanted." The men shook their heads in affirmation as Daxton walked back over to them.

"Let's get you some directions so you and your guys can make landfall under the cover of darkness." Before they went to prepare for their departure, Daxton began using a stick to draw a map in the sand making sure they understood his directions and could find their way back.

Scott was watching Daxton and he told Kelsey. "Daxton is a good man and a born leader. His soul was tortured but he's getting it back day by day. The energy you and Skyler bring him is his best medicine. Even with all this happening now I can still see it."

"Thank you, Scott. And I'm really glad we have you in our lives but I'm here to warn you Daxton already has his hooks in you so you'd better plan on being part of the family from now on."

Standing at six feet, two inches, and two hundred fifty-five pounds of solid muscle, Scott tried to hold his emotions. "I've never had much for family miss, but I've always loved being around you and Skyler and when I met Daxton, I felt the same way. I'm here for all of it. Thank you." Kelsey ran over and gave Scott a hug. He slowly and awkwardly reached around her and hugged her back as Daxton made his way back to them.

"Be careful Scott, you could be number three." Kelsey let Scott go and shot laser eyes at Daxton. "You really have no tact, do you?" She was half-assed serious.

Ignoring Kelsey's comment he said "Okay, well they're heading out and we are about seventy miles by road from where you guys were staying. It's definitely not safe to go back there for a while. Luckily, I spent a little time in this town when I first came here so I know a few folks who can help us lay low for a while.

As Liam's men walked back toward their boat one of them strode over to Kelsey. He handed her a stack of pesos and American money telling her "We always travel with a little extra just in case things like this happen. If you need more, you know how to contact Liam's partner. Al mal tiempo, Buena Cara, you and your family be safe. Take care of each other. He told her as he walked away to board the vessel.

Kelsey looked at Daxton, "What did he just say?"

Daxton turned and looked at the whole group.

"It means that even if we have problems and things go wrong, everything will work out better with a positive attitude. Basically, he was saying that with a smile, everything will look better."

Then he turned and looked toward the town and thought to himself, sure wish someone would have told me that two years ago.

CHAPTER TWENTY NINE

The streetlights flickered in the pouring rain as the four black SUVs made their way down a pothole-filled asphalt road. They followed each other until they pulled into a driveway where a tall steel fence guarded the entrance to a large concrete building. The building was dark, and the only entrance door was along the side.

As the SUVs pulled closer, the gate opened slowly, and they made their way to the facility. They parked in front of the building and the side door opened. A gentleman dressed in black stood in the doorway and held it as the patrons entered through the rain and into the building. They stood in a dimly lit room and shook the water off their jackets and suits. "Please follow me" he directed.

As the man in black approached another door he reached down and placed his thumb on a keypad and the door unlocked. He held the door as they entered, and Mark stood in the middle of the room. "Welcome gentlemen. Please find your seats, they are labeled with your names on them."

"Once you all get seated and comfortable we will begin," Mark said. All the hustle quieted as all the men settled into their assigned seats.

There was a large screen along the back wall. Ten seats and monitors on desks that made a half-moon around a large, covered object. On the screen were seven different choices of language and before Mark began to speak, they changed translation to their own particular languages.

"You were all notified by an outside source, but you are all here for the same reason. To have the opportunity to possess one of the strongest weapons ever designed. Everyone in this room has already made it past the first bidding stage of the process. You are all here now to see the contents in person before you have the opportunity to place your final bid."

The men looked around the room at each other. They were high-ranking officials from all over the world.

"On the desk in front of you, there is a small numerical keyboard. When it is time, you can adjust your bid accordingly. We also have others, as you can see on the monitors, that could not be here today but will be remotely bidding. You already have the facts about the items. You know the history. All the questions have been answered so, that being said, let's go ahead and begin." A light shined brighter over the draped object as Mark walked over and slowly slid the black sheet from the box. As the sheet slid off the amber glistened inside the large clear case.

"As stated here are the four panels that include the code to unlock the design schematics. And as you know the journal holds the plans to complete the build." Mark reminded them.

None of the men could help but stare at what was in front of them. Regardless of where they were from or their backgrounds, they all knew the story. They knew the history. They started typing on their keyboards and the information was shown on the large screen as to who had made the highest bid. As they watched the bids change one of the men asked a question.

"May I have my curator walk in for a closer look at the items?" The translation came across the screen.

"Yes, he may but he must not touch the glass. It will set off the first stage of alarms." Mark answered.

The man nodded his head and motioned for his curator to approach the box. He walked around looking at the panels from all angles. He pulled his glasses from his pocket and slid them onto his face. He leaned in and started closely inspecting the stamped lettering. He slowly reached into his back pocket and pulled out a small, folded piece of paper. He unfolded the paper and looked at the lettering and numbering on it. He looked back at the amber panels more closely. After looking at everything carefully he shook his head. The bidder raised his eyebrow and motioned for his curator to return to his desk. When he returned, he bent down and had a conversation in a whisper in a language that Mark could not interpret. The man looked up at his curator and asked him one more time in English, "Are you sure about this?"

The curator shook his head, yes.

The man at the desk started typing on his keyboard and the translation began coming up on the large wall screen. Mark turned around and looked up at the screen. His attitude changed instantly as he looked back at the man who was typing.

"You come into my place of business after I have invited you here and accuse me of presenting a fake! How the fuck do you get off coming in here and insulting me and the others that have come to secure this priceless item.! The man did not look up but kept typing as Mark yelled and got closer to him.

"I'm fucking talking to you!" Mark pulled his pistol from the back of his waistline and aimed it at the gentleman's face.

At the same time Mark pulled and aimed his gun, three others stood up from the desks along with the curator and drew their weapons. They were all yelling in different languages. "Imposter! Fraud! Fake! Kill him! American idiot asshole!"

Marksmen poured in from the side door with their assault weapons drawn into action position. "Everyone stops! Now! Do it now!" After checking the reaction of the others and the first man had holstered his weapon, the rest slowly followed suit.

Mark's senses were overloaded, and his mind was spinning. He could no longer hear the background noise as he turned around and looked at the large screen. Typed on the screen was every flaw, and inconsistency of the panels that the curator had noted. The curator had also descrambled the top line of the codes on panel one. Mark read it out loud. "Go fuck yourself!" Mark pursed his lips and screamed out loud.

"Mateo, you son of a bitch! I'm going to kill you with my bare hands!"

CHAPTER THIRTY

"What do you think he's burning in that barrel Mom?"

Kelsey made a wide walk around the man and the smoldering barrel. Daxton looked back at them as they walked toward the small town.

"Probably our dinner, so don't knock it too hard," he said.

Skyler looked at Kelsey and asked, "Do you think he's serious Mom?" Kelsey shook her head as she sped up and closed the gap between her and Daxton. "Hey Dax, honestly, what are we going to do here? What is our plan? We have our daughter to think about." Daxton was quiet for a moment before he stopped in the middle of the trail. "Look Kels, I'm just about as perplexed about this situation as you are. I'm just playing out scenarios in my head now trying to figure out our next move and what's going to keep us all safe."

About that time a young Hispanic woman ran over to Scott and grabbed his bicep. "Oooh, so nice. Big muscles and so handsome." Scott began to turn red. "You amigo, Daxton?" The young woman said.

Kelsey shook her head. "Why is it you know absolutely every woman that we come have into contact with?"

"Si Rosa, mi amigo, Scott." Daxton turned his head and winked at Rosa as she walked next to Scott as close as she possibly could. "It must be a thing Kels, I just get along with the opposite sex I guess."

Kelsey rolled her eyes as a young man approached Daxton. He walked directly up to him and got into his face talking loudly," Where's my money? I want my money now!" He pushed Daxton and Scott broke free from Rosa's grip and made his way to them.

"I have no problem with you big man. This guy owes me money!"

Daxton reached over and put the man in a headlock and scrubbed his head with his knuckles. "Yeah, you want your money, Manuel? Well, you owe me for drinking all my damn beer last time! And you're damn sure the worst poker player I've ever met!" Daxton let the young man go and kicked him in the ass. The man spun around and grabbed Daxton for a hug.

"Good to see you, Mr. Dax, you still owe me twelve bucks. Your Familia?" he pointed at everyone.

"Twelve bucks? It was four you dirty little thief!" Daxton laughed.

"Interest my friend," Manuel replied.

"Si, Mi family, Manuel this is Kelsey my ex… or…or something….my wife." Daxton stammered. And this is my beautiful daughter, Skyler, my adopted brother, Scott, and our new friend Mateo." Daxton said introducing each of them to Manuel.

Manuel made the rounds with each of them introducing himself as only Manuel could do. He stopped with Skyler and kissed her hand. "Bonita, Muy Bonita." Daxton picked up a stick and tossed it at Manuel's legs. Manuel jumped and dodged the stick.

"If you want to live to collect your four dollars, Manuel, I suggest you back off!"

Everyone chuckled as Manuel moved back toward Daxton.

"Yes, yes Mr. Dax So, you never said how long you would be here, so I didn't know how many supplies to have ready for you. I didn't know you would have more people as well. But we will make it work for you.

Kelsey caught up with Daxton. "You planned this? You planned on coming here after you did what Liam needed you to do? I don't understand!"

"I needed a backup plan, Kelsey. I knew Liam wasn't the only one that knew what was in that case. It was too high profile. He spent millions on that sub and arranging all this. You can't have a full-blown operation with it going unnoticed. I had no idea it would play out like this, but I did know that we would all need a place to lay low for a while if shit went down. Here we are. Shit went down." Daxton did his best to explain.

Kelsey was quiet for a few moments. "Thank you. Thank you for protecting our daughter. I shouldn't have let her come Daxton. It's my fault we are all here. I'm so sorry." Daxton turned and grabbed her by the shoulders.

"That is the last time I want to hear you take the blame for this Kelsey Shaw. Period. I agreed to take this job on for Liam and you know damn well you weren't getting out of the country without Skyler coming along. Can I tell you something?"

Kelsey nodded. "What scares the hell out of me is that if I had said no to this it would have been someone else. Someone who doesn't love you and Skyler like I do. He wouldn't die to make sure you were both okay. And here we are. And Kels....... we will make it out of this."

All that Kelsey heard was that Daxton still loved her. Her knees got weak, and she shut her eyes tightly as a tear ran down her cheek. Daxton took his thumb and wiped the tear away. He looked around to where Manuel stood, already telling stories about him.

He yelled, "Hey, Hemingway! Leave them alone and let's get everyone something to eat and drink. They'll have plenty of time to hear your stories. It's been a really long day for us all."

CHAPTER THIRTY ONE

Manuel walked in front of them as they made their way through the main street of the small village. "My amigos, Mr. Dax made it back to see us!" he said to some patrons sitting in front of a small makeshift cantina. The ones who knew Daxton stood up and greeted him and he introduced them to all the others in his group.

Manuel shuffled away from the table and back out into the street with Daxton and the rest following behind. "Tonight, we have dinner at mi casa. Mi espousa has prepared a very nice dinner in case you did make it back this evening." Daxton put his hand on Manuel's shoulder. "We don't want to intrude or disrupt your familia, my friend."

"Oh no, she insists! I told her I didn't want you in my house because you smell bad and scare the children, but she insisted I not argue." Manuel joked.

They all chuckled and gave Daxton sideways grins while he told Manuel, "Well, if she insisted then that's what we will do, but I probably do smell bad." Daxton also laughed at Manuel's joke.

Inside Manuel's home, his small children played on the floor and amazing smells flowed from the kitchen. Manuel's wife came out and hugged everyone and welcomed them into their home. She grabbed Skyler and looked into her eyes and then looked back at Daxton.

"This poor baby looks just like her father. But she is much more beautiful. Please find a seat and food will be ready soon." She smiled.

They all found a place at the table and sat down as Manuel's wife made her way back to the kitchen. Daxton walked over to where Manuel's baby daughter played lifted her up and set her on his hip.

"So, Manuel, tell me how you came to meet Daxton?" Kelsey asked. Manuel smiled and became quiet. "Well Miss, he just kinda wandered into our village. I was out picking up some loose debris, you see, we had winds coming in early the next morning. It was late and I was going to walk to my house when I saw swerving headlights coming up the jungle road. This gringo had his radio turned up and was listening to some white boy rock and roll. I watched as he slowly went past me, and he waved. He seemed very friendly and very out of place. As he was waving and drinking from his beer he drove right into the ocean. I mean all the way up to the doors before he even stopped. He calmly got out of the Jeep as the headlights pierced the waves underwater. With his beer still in his hand he wandered back over to me. He reached out his hand for a shake and said sorry about your ocean, I'm Daxton Shaw. He asked me if there was another beer anywhere in this town." Everyone laughed and Kelsey just shook her head.

"He seemed so nice, so I took him to my covered porch and sat him down in a chair. I had my friend pull his Jeep out of the ocean and spray it off. He ended up drinking all of my beer, but we visited all night about you and your daughter and his adventures. I mentioned to him that my mother was dying in Las Vegas, and I wished I could see her before she passed away. He told me to let him sleep for a couple of hours and to go pack a bag. When the sun rose, I went outside to check on him. He was shirtless, sitting on the beach just watching the sunrise all alone. I took him some coffee and we visited about families as it became full daylight."

"Aw, come on Manuel" Daxton interrupted. "You make it sound like some sort of romance novel!" Manuel chuckled as did the others.

"Anyway, Manuel continued. "We loaded up into his Jeep after hours of getting it to crank and he took me to his plane. He took a shower in the water hose and changed and the next thing I knew we flew to Las Vegas. I never fly before but I was happy, not nervous. Mr. Daxton waited for me there for three days as my mother passed away. I got to be with her and my baby sister in her last moments of life. He flew us home and then drove me back to my house where we sat. My family has been in debt to him since then. I wish he would have taken my money instead of him keep coming here and drinking up all my cervezas though." Manuel walked by Daxton and pushed him on the shoulder and they both laughed. Kelsey looked down and held back tears once again. She knew Daxton was the best man she'd ever met and the fact that he was hurting so much was ripping her heart into pieces.

It was then that Manuel's wife appeared from the kitchen.

"Comamos mi familia" she said as she walked in holding a giant plate.

Daxton and Manuel sat back down at the table. There was conversation and laughter as well as amazing food to satisfy their hunger. Their troubles took a back seat for the time being and Kelsey could not help but stare at Daxton.

Skyler watched placed her hand on Kelsey's leg, and said to her, "He's going to be okay Mom. We're going to take Dad home with us."

CHAPTER THIRTY TWO

As they wrapped up dinner Skyler and Kelsey found their way into the kitchen to help with the dishes. "No, no, no" Manuel's wife insisted. "You are guests in mi casa. No work, just relax."

"Please let us help you, dinner was amazing, and we can't let you do this all alone," Kelsey replied.

Manuel's wife thought about it for a moment and then handed them both rags to help. As they picked up and hand-washed the dishes Manuel's wife, Minosa, looked at Kelsey. "El Esposo is a good man. He helps Manuel and me with the English. He brings Manuel magazines and brings me good groceries from the town I don't get here. He is good to bambinos and brings them birthday gifts."

Kelsey and Skyler smiled. "Thank you Minosa for taking him in and making him your friend. You are very nice people for helping us."

Minosa laughed as she pulled another dish from the sink. "No just us, everyone here take Mr. Daxton as family. He hurting but he smile more now than before."

Just as Kelsey was getting ready to respond Manuel walked into the kitchen and speaking to Kelsey and Skyler said, "Okay Bonita we go to your rooms now. You are tired and Mucho belly full!" He rubbed his stomach.

Kelsey and Skyler hugged Minosa deeply and could tell without words how genuine she really was.

"Breakfast tomorrow early. Or coffee for Mr. Daxton." She told them. Kelsey nodded and she and Skyler followed Manuel into the living room. Daxton was kissing babies on their heads when he saw them come into the room. Scott, Mateo, and Daxton walked into the kitchen to give Minosa hugs and their gratitude.

They made their exit following Manuel down the small gravel road toward a concrete building. They went up a flight of stairs and Manuel opened the door. "We have blankets and sheets and there is fresh water on the desk there for you. It is no vacation home, but we have for four days if you need."

Daxton hugged Manuel and shook his hand, "Thank you, my friend. There are no other words to say thank you. But thank you!" Manuel winked at Daxton and showed everyone their sleeping arrangement.

Daxton went to the couch, "I'll sit up here, I've been used to sleeping on the couch for years."

Kelsey walked by him and shoulder-checked him. "That mouth of yours is exactly what put you on the couch for those years.' Daxton shook his head.

Manuel said his goodbyes and left the small home. Daxton sat on the couch, reached down, and started unlacing his boots. "Man, it's hell getting old!"

"You should have been in the gym these last two years instead of the bars. Kelsey and Daxton always gave each other a hard time as they both had a competitive nature. It was never ill-willed but just a part of their relationship.

"You sure are on fire tonight Kels! Glad there's a door to your room so I don't have to listen to you yappin'!" He quipped.

Skyler dawned a huge smile and looked at Kelsey. This is what she remembered growing up. The playful banter and traveling to crazy places together.

Mateo sat down on his bed and rested his face in the palm of his hands. Scott laid back in his bed adjusting his pillow behind his head. "You have been very quiet all day. Is everything okay?" Scott said as he looked over at Mateo.

Mateo took a deep breath before he answered. "They will go after my family. I made them go to a safer place, but Mark and the others will find them. He threatened their lives and when he finds out the artifacts have been stolen, he will be looking for them and for me."

Scott sat up. "We will figure this out. I'm sure your family will be safe. I feel you are a smart man and would move them to a location where they would be hard to find."

"I am really hoping so," Mateo said as he laid back into his bed. "Goodnight, I am going to try to get some rest if I can. I'm thinking we will need all we can get." Scott nodded slipped his hat down over his eyes and crossed his arms.

Daxton pulled his boots off and walked into Kelsey and Skyler's room. "If you two need anything come and get me. If anyone comes through that door you guys go out the back."

Skyler got up and gave Daxton a hug. "I love you, Dad." Kelsey smiled and pulled the pillow underneath her head. Daxton walked over and kissed her without even thinking, it was like second nature, and he had done it a million times before. After he had kissed her forehead, he realized what he had done. "I didn't mean to make that awkward, it's just a habit. I …." Before Daxton could speak another word Kelsey's gorgeous glassy green eyes stared back at him.

"It's okay Daxton. It was sweet and one thing I'm glad you didn't forget. Thank you for saving my life today." She slowly closed her eyes, but she didn't immediately go to sleep.

Daxton tapped Skyler's foot. "Goodnight, Kiddo. Sweet dreams, love you." She answered with a "Night Dad, love you too,"

As Kelsey lay on her bed and listened to the small fan blow, she couldn't help but think of Daxton. Even with the events that had taken place all she could think about were the amazing times they'd all had as a family.

CHAPTER THIRTY THREE

    Kelsey's eyes opened to sunbeams dancing off the edge of the tattered metal blinds that partially covered the window. She looked around, forgetting for a moment where she was. She looked over at Skyler's bed. It was made and obviously, she was already up and moving. She stretched and got out of bed, quickly dressed, and peeked into Mateo and Scott's room as she was passing. They were also up and gone. She walked into the small kitchen, and she could smell the fresh coffee brewing. As she approached the coffee maker, she saw there was a note beside it. She picked up the note and smiled. It read: "Thank you for being alive today. At the beach." -Dax. Daxton used to write her notes when he brought her coffee in the mornings. He was always up long before Kelsey was. She poured her coffee and walked out the door and down the steps. She could see Daxton and Skyler sitting on the beach near the water talking and laughing. She smiled and took a sip from her coffee as the sun warmed her face.

"Morning Mrs. Kelsey," Scott said, slightly out of breath as he rounded the corner.

"Good morning, Scott, out for your morning run as usual I see," she replied.

"You know I'm not gonna miss! This big boy gotta run to keep the blood flowing, that and work off some of Minosa's good cooking!"

Realizing that Kelsey was watching Daxton and Skyler he remarked, "Those two were already gone when I came out."

"Can I ask you something, Mrs. Kelsey?"

"You know you always can Scott. You have been there for me and Sky for a long time." Kelsey answered.

"How come you never spoke about Daxton? In the last couple of years, I may have heard his name only a half dozen times until recently. He has a heart of gold and is a good dude."

"You know Scott, I thought maybe it would be easier if I just blocked out the past and didn't talk about him. When he left, I begged and pleaded for him to get help. I texted, I called, and checked on him. But as time passed and he would disappear so did my worries about him. It wasn't that I didn't care, but I had to keep it together for Skyler. I could have just as easily ended up as Daxton did. I realize what he went through was nothing like I was dealing with, but it was a struggle losing him."

"I can imagine and understand. I know it had to be hard on you. I am sorry to pry." Scott felt bad for asking.

Kelsey told him, "No, no, it's okay. Thank you for always being there Scott. You have always been good to me and Skyler.

"I think you need to go down there with them Mrs. Kelsey."

Kelsey smiled at Scott and headed down through the sand and to the oceanside to join Daxter and Skyler.

"Hey, you two! Did you even sleep at all?" she jokingly asked.

Skyler chuckled, rolled her eyes, and said. "Yes, Mom, but we don't lay around until noon to get our beauty sleep."

Daxton said, "Leave your Mom alone Sky. We both know she needs all the beauty rest she can get."

Kelsey laughed, shook her head, and sat down Indian style between them. "I understand why you came down here Dax. The sunrise, the smell, the air, and the people."

About that time a young woman in a bikini came jogging in front of them. "Obviously, the women down here don't wear many clothes either," she added. "Anyway, what are we doing today? What is the plan and what are we going to do about all of this?"

Daxton picked up a handful of sand and slowly let it trickle out of his fist and back to the beach. "Well, Mateo told me this morning that he knows where the real case is back on the island. He thinks Mark will go after his family after he finds out that his case is a fake. We're going to lay low for two days and then go back to the island and get the case. Mateo knows where the case needs to go so it doesn't get into the hands of the wrong people. He's also afraid that if we make a call to anyone Mark will intercept somehow."

"He's not sure what to do about his family but it sounds like he has them in a safe place for now. I really feel for him. I can't imagine not knowing. Regardless, we are lying low today and tomorrow. There's a waterfall just about three and a half miles up the side of that small mountain over there." he said pointing. "I say we go see Minosa to grab some snacks and head up there to check it out."

"Hiking Dax, you really think we should be out doing that today?

"We don't need to be seen around town but if you just want to lay around and drink beer all day, I've been the reigning champion of just that down here for two years," Daxton said sadly. "I need to keep busy Kelsey," he said in explanation.

Kelsey understood and said, "Hiking sounds perfect!"

"Kels, I don't want to bring it up, but do you think we need to tell someone about Liam?"

"No, it's okay. Liam knew what he was doing, and he knew the risks. The men that came and got us will clean up the mess and make something up for his family, I'm sure. I'm grateful for what he did for me and Skyler, but I am not in mourning over it or him. Men have died for real causes, and it goes unnoticed, by our friends and family who served. He was a trafficker and nothing else. I just pray for his family and that's it. Let's just go hike."

Daxton opened his eyes wide at Skyler and she did the same back to him. Kelsey was a very strong woman, and it was hard to get her rattled. She was done talking about him and that was that.

"Okay then Kels, let's go hike," he told her and Skyler.

Daxton, Kelsey, and Skyler got up brushed the sand off themselves, and headed toward Manuel's house.

"Hey, Dad."

"Yes, Skyler?" Daxton said.

"Don't go chasing waterfalls, please stick to the river and the streams that your used too."

"Jesus, Sky, you are definitely my daughter, so where's your sense of adventure?" Daxton teased her.

The three of them laughed as they followed the path back to the house to prepare to spend the day together in the jungle.

CHAPTER THIRTY FOUR

Daxton pulled his knife out of its sheath and began cutting an orange into smaller slices. He tossed a slice into his mouth as he loaded the small plastic bag with the fresh fruit. He stood at the kitchen counter shirtless, prepping as Kelsey stepped in and she couldn't help but stare. "I see that you still don't believe in shirts or clothes like the rest of us," Kelsey said.

Daxton smiled and said, "Don't come at me woman, I saw your bathing suit. I hope you didn't pay much for that!"

Kelsey opened the fridge as she chuckled. "Whatever!

"How many waters do you want me to grab Dax? I feel like this is the last thing we need to be doing today but I guess you're right. Need to keep our heads straight and our bodies in motion." As she talked, she couldn't peel her eyes off Daxton. "Look, I don't know what kind of diet you've been doing but damn Daxton I'm not going to lie. You look amazing. I have no clue how you do it."

Daxton acted like he was putting a drink in his mouth. "Twelve-ounce curls baby! Boom." Kelsey put her face in her hands and shook her head.

"Anyway, thank you and don't you ever change Kels. Gorgeous and toned up as always. Always hated keeping up with you so you didn't ditch me for someone else. Daxton winked at her. "And a couple of bottles each should do. It's not too intense a trek. Did you see Scott and Mateo? Are they going to hang around here today?"

"They are going to stay here today. I asked them if they wanted to come but they said there was no way, for us to go ahead without them." Kelsey answered.

Skyler came bursting through the door. She went over to Daxton and hugged him around the neck. "Minosa told me that you freaking delivered her baby! What the hell Dad, that's so badass and why didn't you ever tell me that? Is there anything you can't do? I love you and thank you for taking us hiking today. And Minosa gave us these tamales to take." She tossed them to Daxton.

He said," Oh my God, these are amazing Sky, wait until you get a taste of these! Mmmmm hmmmmm!"

Kelsey gazed at Daxton. "A baby Daxton" Seriously? Someone let you assist in delivering a baby?"

Daxton shrugged his shoulders. "No one else wanted to try so I figured I'd take a shot at it. Baby and Mama both lived, right? Hell, and I was half a bottle of tequila in" he said under his breath. He grabbed a pillow from the couch and pulled the pillowcase off. He got some rope he had found earlier and started tying hoops and affixed the pillowcase.

He slid his arms through the hoops and the pillowcase was positioned on his back. "Wala! Instant backpack!"

Kelsey grinned and had that amused look she did when he came up with his unusual ideas.

"Well here, put all this in your fancy backpack" She threw a water bottle at him.

Skyler came back into the room as Daxton loaded the backpack and said, "Cool backpack Dad,"

Daxton winked at Kelsey.

Alright, crew let's leave our troubles behind and go enjoy the day. God knows we need a break. They finished getting ready and headed out the door.

"Guess your shirt isn't going to make the trip with us?" Kelsey said as they walked down the steps.

They all laughed and joked as they got to the entrance of the trail.

Daxton pointed up. "That's where we are headed," he told them. "It's been a minute, but I think I can get us up there to the waterfall and back without getting us too lost."

The trio hiked up the small dirt trail and Skyler pushed ahead a little out of listening range. Kelsey and Daxton touched hands and looked at each other.

"Daxton, what happened? I know you've been through some really dark times and were not yourself but since we've been down here and even with all this you seem well.... happy again.

Like the man I fell in love with. And every day you seem just better than the day before."

Daxton reached over and grabbed Kelsey's hand. She squeezed it ever so tightly.

"It's you and Skyler. It's having a purpose again, having you guys count on me to be here. I had a dream and a full-on awakening not that very long ago, actually it was right before you guys came down. After that and after spending time with you guys, I'll never go back to the way I was living. I was a hollow shell repeating the same thing daily. Running from what made me the happiest man on the planet. There is no more running, there is no more drinking for the wrong reasons, and there is only peace and happiness going forward. I am so sorry for what I have put you and Skyler through, Kelsey. And regardless of how things work out I am coming back stateside and will be there for you and Skyler. I have no plans. I have no ideas, but I do know I want to be involved in Skyler's life."

Kelsey looked at Daxton with tears in her eyes. "What about me Daxton? Where do I fit into this?"

Daxton reached up and wiped her tears away. He grabbed her by the back of the arms and pulled her to him.

He kissed her lips deeply and passionately and then pulled away. "Ugh, I'm sorry Kels, I didn't mean to.... Before Daxton could speak another word, she threw her arms around his neck and went back for a longer kiss. She hugged him tightly and kissed him just as she did when he used to return from a long trip.

Skyler had turned to ask a question to see them kissing and holding onto each other. Her smile was so big it could have been seen from space. Kelsey and Daxton stared into each other's eyes and held hands.

"Go, Dad! Woo hoo!" Skyler yelled from the trail above them.

Daxton and Kelsey smiled, both a little embarrassed like it was the first time they'd ever kissed. Daxton turned red.

"Well, look at you Mr. Shaw, the legend actually does get embarrassed now doesn't he!" Kelsey grinned as she teased him. Daxton shook his head saying "It's the sun, so bright out here today. I just tan easily."

Kelsey burst into laughter and said, "The sun hasn't come out all morning Dax!"

Skyler yelled back at them. "Come on lovebirds! I want to see that waterfall sometime this year!" She backtracked the short distance to them and wrapped her hand around Daxton's as the three of them made the rest of their way up the trail

Skyler, after a brief time, went out in front to give her parents a little space and time to talk. Kelsey still had her pinky finger wrapped around Daxton's as they walked the dirt path.

"So, exactly how many bracelets does one man need these days Mr. Shaw?" Kelsey ran her hand across Daxton's wrist.

Daxton had acquired some bracelets from the local kids and a few women friends along the way in the last couple of years.

"Well, I guess if you must know, I have a hard time giving them away. Most of the locals have made them and when I see them, they always check to see if I'm still wearing the one that they gave me. So, I feel like I have to, so they know that I value their gift."

Kelsey took a deep breath. "You know Dax. the one thing you have managed to keep is that big ass heart of yours. I'm glad that didn't fade. Can I ask a question, Dax?"

"Go ahead, shoot," he said.

"If it hadn't been for that plane crash and all the events it led to, where do you think we would be in our lives?"

Daxton blew out a deep breath. "You know half of the reason I would try to numb the pain is so that very question in my head would go away. I asked myself that daily, more than once a day. How could we all just be a family, happy and together, but that's not how it played out. And that's not the hand I was dealt. If I could have changed anything about that day I would go back in a minute."

Kelsey was about to speak when Skyler turned around and yelled, "Hey Dad, I'm getting hungry. Can we stop and have a couple of tamales?" as she looked back at Daxton and Kelsey to see they were still holding hands.

"Dude, you eat more than all of us combined, Sky! Where do you pack it all? We'll be there in about twenty minutes and the view for lunch will be so much better there I promise you."

Skyler threw her arms up into the air. "Fine, but if I pass out from starvation you will just have to carry me."

Daxton laughed as he looked at Kelsey. "Wonder where she gets the theatrics from?' Daxton looked up into the trees. He knew damn well it wasn't from Kelsey.

The trio hiked for the next fifteen minutes or so laughing and talking and soon they could hear the water off in the distance.

When Skyler heard the waterfall, she immediately picked up the pace and left Daxton and Kelsey behind.

Kelsey kissed Daxton on the cheek and took off after Skyler.

Daxton had a huge grin after he started running after the two of them. When he finally caught up and rounded a corner Kelsey and Skyler were already standing underneath a small section of the waterfall.

"Daxton, It's gorgeous here! You were totally right! Kelsey said as she ran her hands through her hair as the water fell down on top of her.

"C'mon Dad, get in." Skyler invited. Daxton slipped off his shoes and shallow dove into the water. He swam over to them and splashed Skyler like he always did when they were in the water. Skyler jumped on him, and he twisted her into a lock hold,

"You know you'll never get the jump on Dad kiddo! But you just keep on trying" They laughed, and he let her go. Alright, hotshot, follow me." Daxton made his way over toward the rock wall. "Alright Sky, watch my hand and foot placement," he instructed. Daxton started his climb as Kelsey started coming toward them,

"Absolutely not Daxton Shaw! No! Sky, do not follow him up there!" But it was too late, Skyler was already five feet behind him and heading up the thirty-foot wall.

"I'm good Mom, calm down! Always the negative Nancy!"

Kelsey looked down at the water and shook her head. She put her hand on the rocks and started after Daxton and Skyler.

Daxton looked below him at Skyler and Kelsey. "Looky there Skyler! Even Mom came to the party! Okay, easy and slow guys, the rocks can be slippery."

They got to the top of the waterfall and Daxton pointed down to the water and said, "See that hole right there? That's what we're aiming for!" Daxton pointed at the deeper section of the water.

"Jesus, Dax! Really?!" Kelsey groaned.

'Aww come on Mom! It's not that far down there." Skyler said as she looked over the edge.

"Fine, but I'm counting down!" Kelsey reached both of her hands out and Daxton and Skyler grabbed them. "Okay, on one we jump. Three..two..one!" They threw themselves off the jagged-edged cliff and all hit the water at the same time. One by one their heads popped through the surface.

"Whoa! That was awesome!" Skyler yelled while she looked around her. When she turned, she saw her Mom and Dad wrapped up underneath the waterfalls kissing passionately.

"Get a room!" she yelled and laughed.

"Mind your own business Sky!" Kelsey yelled to Skyler and turned back to Daxton telling him, "I've been wanting to do that for two years." She winked at him and swam off toward Skyler.

Daxton followed closely behind and swam up to them. "Alright, my ladies, we have about ten minutes to hang out then we need to make our way back. Minosa will have our asses if we're late for dinner. They spent the last few minutes swimming around the gorgeous waterfall as it glimmered in the sunlight surrounded by the jungle canopy of Mexico.

CHAPTER THIRTY FIVE

Kelsey made her way through the tall grass toward the makeshift runway. Daxton stood bent over in front of the engine cowling area on the small aircraft.

"Excuse me good lookin', are you qualified to work on that thing, mister?" Kelsey teased.

Daxton turned around holding a piece of the motor. "You have impeccable timing! I need an extra set of hands. Here, hold this." He handed Kelsey the part as he wiped his brow with his wrist. He kissed her forehead and reached down to get his ratchet from the tool bag. "Well, Kels, as I see it I'm probably the most qualified in this town. Although you may not have much faith in my aircraft mechanical skills, it's all ya' got honey." He smiled and continued working on the airplane. He wrenched on the motor and spoke at the same time.

"We're going to need this girl to get us out of here Kels and we are literally down to the ounce of weight capacity that she can take. Half of the damned weight is our ol' corn-fed buddy." Kelsey laughed and shook her head in agreement.

"I drained half the fuel out just to make room for his overgrown ass." Daxton reached his hand back over toward Kelsey for the part and he went back to work.

"How much longer have you got Dax?" Kelsey asked. "Minosa is cooking us dinner tonight. Can I tell you that I don't want to leave here? I'm scared of what is back home and I love it here already."

Daxton placed his ratchet down on the plane and turned around to catch Kelsey in a hug. "Kelsey, I don't know where home is or what it even looks like at this point, but I do know that my home is right in front of me. You and Sky are home Kels. I can't promise you where that will be on the map but when we make it out of here, which we will, we will all be together in that place."

Tears ran like a faucet down Kelsey's face. She pursed her lips and shook her head that she agreed. "I want that. I want that more than anything Dax. I love you and there hasn't been a moment when I didn't since we met."

The light breeze gently swayed the tall blades of grass as the sun gleamed from the backside of the mountain ridge. Daxton held Kelsey in an embrace. They could each feel the emotions of the other while they stood there.

Kelsey helped Daxton wrap up the final touches on the aircraft and they headed back to Manuel and Minosa's for dinner.

Daxton knocked on the door, he could hear Skyler laughing and he smiled at Kelsey. "That girl can make friends with a damn fence post!"

Kelsey gave Daxton the look and replied with a grin, "And where in the world do you think she might have picked that up?"

Manuel opened the door leaned over to give Kelsey a hug and kiss on the cheek and asked, "Why'd you bring this street bum with you?"

Manuel punched Daxton in the arm and then gave him a big bear hug. "Please come in mi hermano!"

As Daxton entered, he looked over at Skyler. She had the baby bouncing on her hip as she shook a small stuffed turtle around in the air. The house was filled with the most amazing smells and Mexican music could be heard coming from the kitchen.

"Aww, come here, it's my turn now!" Kelsey said as she held her hands out for the baby.

Daxton walked into the kitchen area and Scott and Mateo stood at the island helping prepare dinner alongside Minosa.

Manual reached into the refrigerator and brought out two more beers. Kelsey watched him pop the tops and hand the beers to Daxton and Scott. "Hey, can I ask you to make me one of those as well, if it's not too much trouble?" she said as she walked into the kitchen with the baby.

"Make it two more," Skyler said as she walked in behind Kelsey.

Minosa walked from behind the island and kissed Daxton and Kelsey.

As the beers were being passed out Manuel said, "Let's all gather around for a toast." Everyone huddled close to the island and Manuel raised his beer into the air saying, "A mi Familia le espera amor y adventura" Then he translated to English, "To my family, love and adventure awaits!"

They clanked their beers together in the air. "Salud!"

As they took sips of their beer, Minosa signaled for everyone to start taking things to the table. Everyone picked up a dish and went to the large wooden dining table. As it was being set, Kelsey placed the baby on her blanket, and everyone gathered around the table.

"Shall we pray for this meal? Manuel asked. "No?"

" Daxton will lead prayer Esta Noche" Manuel nodded his head.

"Mr. Daxton, it is all yours, mi amigo."

Daxton looked around at his family and friends. "Spanish or English?" he asked.

Manuel said, "Let's do English this evening."

Daxton nodded his head and reached for Skyler and Kelsey's hands as he bowed his head. Everyone was connected by hands as Daxton prayed.

"Dear Heavenly Father, I want to thank you for this beautiful meal that our families have prepared together. I want to thank you for the warm hearts of Manuel and Minosa and for allowing us to gain these new family members that we will cherish forever. I thank you personally for clearing my thoughts and showing me the path to happiness and love again. And for the opportunity to have these two beautiful women in my life.

Last but not least, please do not judge us for what we may do tomorrow but yet, guide us to safety and keep watch over us, In the Lord's name I pray, Amen."

They conversed and enjoyed the amazing meal that Minosa had cooked once again for them but in the back of their minds, they were all still thinking about their return to Palm Island the very next day.

CHAPTER THIRTY SIX

The small panga cut through the only beach sand shoreline on the island. Mateo pulled the motor up as Scott jumped off the front of the boat. Scott grabbed one of the lines and threw it up over his shoulder dug his heels deep into the sand and pulled the boat up further onto the beach.

"You guys jump out and I'll hand you our gear," Daxton said as he placed all their gear on one side of the small boat. Kelsey, Skyler, and Mateo each jumped into the warm sand and Scott pulled the boat even further onto the beach. He tied the line to a piece of large driftwood and went to help the others unload.

Mateo handed Kelsey a small bag telling her, "You're in charge of this. It's anti-venom. Don't let it out of your sight." Scott got closer and heard the directions Mateo gave Kelsey. "Anti-venom for what?" he asked Mateo. "Snakes, this island is covered in snakes. Probably some that haven't been discovered yet." Mateo answered. Kelsey shook her head at Mateo so he would stop the conversation. She remembered a time she had asked Scott if he was ever afraid of anything and he had told her, just snakes, ma'am.

"C'mon, snakes?! Really? With all this other bullshit you're gonna put snakes in the mix too?" Scott pointed down to his tattoo sleeve and his voice rose, "You see this? It's a snake and it reminds me every day how much I hate them!"

Daxton threw him a backpack and said," Come on now big guy. Skyler had a pet snake for two years named Tusa. She was a really nice snake. Ain't that right, Sky?" Skyler chuckled. "I totally forgot about Tusa. She really was a nice snake. She only bit me three times."

Scott shivered and shook his head. "Who the hell owns a snake and what is wrong with you all?"

Kelsey smiled. "We are Shaw's." she winked at Daxton as they unloaded the remainder of the gear.

"Okay boss, so let's get this straight. We're in the middle of the Pacific Ocean, on an island that for some reason isn't on most maps, is circled by hundreds of Tiger sharks and now I find out it's covered in venomous snakes that National Geographic hasn't even identified yet. We're stealing a detailed set of drawings along with a leather journal from Hitler.

Adolf fuckin' Hitler! And, just for fun, some panels from the original Amber room. Let's just go ahead and throw in an undetectable custom-built ROV sub that can cover five thousand miles to haul it all. Maybe a contracted black ops asshole as well that will kill anyone and everyone that gets in his way, ehh? That sums it up. I'm sure I missed a few details so please, fill me in if I am. Scott said sarcastically. Daxton looked at Kelsey, over at Skyler, and then Mateo. "No buddy. I think that pretty much sums it up. Did he miss anything guys? They all shook their head no. Damn, Scott, you haven't said that much since we first met!" Daxton said.

Getting in the last word on the subject Scott let them know he thought they were all certifiably insane as he put their gear on higher ground.

Mateo walked onto the beach as he pulled the GPS from his pocket. He held it up to chest level to get a better signal. He returned to the rest of the group telling them, "We don't have far to go. It's up on the ridge and shouldn't take more than an hour to get up there." They slung the backpacks over their shoulders and slowly made their way from the beach area into the rocky terrain. It was slow going up the steeper portion of the hill in a single file line. Mateo watched the GPS closely. Daxton put his hand into the air signaling for them to stop. "Let's go ahead and take a break and grab a drink. Looks like a good stopping point here."

As they lightened their load by removing the backpacks, Daxton remarked to Skyler, "I cannot believe you still have that backpack, Sky. That thing has been more places than most have seen their whole life, girl!" Daxton took a sip from his bladder hose. Kelsey threw her pack down and sat on a rock next to Mateo as he looked at the GPS.

"She takes it everywhere. I've tried to make her carry actual luggage and she just won't do it. It's that smelly old backpack every time." Skyler pulled her backpack off and placed it on the rock in front of her. "You and Mom had it embroidered for me, and it has all these patches you guys got me. I am not replacing it any time soon!"

As she sat down on the rock behind her, she felt something hit her lower back. She reached back quickly and placed her hand where she instantly started feeling a burning sensation through her side. She stayed quiet as she stood up and looked behind her. A green snake lay under a branch looking back at her and then it slithered away. "Dad…. Dad" Her hand slipped off her back slowly and Daxton could see the two small holes, and fang marks on her side. He caught her as her knees buckled and she folded forward.

"Kelsey, give me the anti-venom now!" Daxton yelled as he rolled her over.

"Dad, tell me I'm okay. Please, Dad, tell me," Skyler pleaded.

Daxton reassured her, "You're going to be okay, baby. I got you, haven't I always? Skyler shook her head as Kelsey fumbled through the bag for the anti-venom. She talked to Skyler as she did "We got you Sky, hold tight baby. Your Dad and I are here baby. Just breathe and stay calm." Kelsey was trying to keep Skyler from panicking. She grabbed the anti-venom bag and threw it to Daxton. Scott jumped up and hovered over Skyler while Mateo looked to make sure the snake was gone. Kelsey held her hand as Daxton opened the bag and put the injection kit into his hand.

"How do we know what this is for? Is it even the right anti-venom? Mateo, can I give this to her?" Daxton questioned.

Mateo, flustered, answered "It's a viper anti-venom. They say all snakes are some kind of vipers. Just do it Daxton!"

Daxton looked up at Mateo and shook his head. He hesitated.

"Let's go in a vein, give me that!" Kelsey grabbed the injector from Daxton. "Okay baby, you're going to be okay. Hold her hands as tightly as you can. "

Skyler squeezed Scott and Daxton's hands tightly as Kelsey stuck Skyler directly into the vein of her arm. "Okay baby, it's going to take a little time to start working."

Skyler's breathing was becoming very shallow. She could hear everyone talking and trying to keep her awake, but her eyelids began to close, and the sun's rays turned to darkness. She could feel her heartbeat and her body tightening but there was absolutely nothing she could do.

    She lay on her back on the rock while they all gathered around her. The toxic venom pulsed through her veins. Only time would be able to diagnose the outcome.

CHAPTER THIRTY SEVEN

"Skyler! Skyler! Come on, baby. Open your eyes, talk to us." Kelsey yelled as she held Skyler's hand.

Skyler could hear her mother yelling and see light coming through the bottom of her eyelids. She couldn't feel her arms or legs but as the seconds ticked by, she began to flutter her eyelids and take deeper breaths.

"Oh my God, baby, can you hear me? Squeeze my hand if you can baby." Kelsey wailed.

Skyler concentrated as she began to feel her mother touching and holding her hand. She focused and managed to move her fingers just enough to let Kelsey know she was conscious.

"She's squeezing my hand, Daxton! I can feel her trying to squeeze my hand! Baby, I'm here, we are all here." Kelsey yelled.

Skyler could feel her arms start to tingle and could wiggle her toes. Her eyes opened as Daxton was bending down to kiss her forehead.

"Sky, listen to me, baby. You are going to be okay. We got you. Just relax and breathe for us, okay?"

Skyler took deeper breaths and could feel her muscles starting to fire back up. She was tingling all over and felt as if needles were running over her body. She squeezed Kelsey's hand harder and harder as time passed. She took one more deep breath and rolled her head toward Daxton and quietly managed to say, "Did you bite that friggin" snake back for me?" In between tears, they laughed as they both embraced Skyler.

Scott got up, turned around, and threw his hands into the air. "You are all completely insane!" He wiped his own tears away. He had to also take some deep breaths.

Skyler slowly gained motor functions back and the tingling was fading. "He took off before I could get a good clean bite out of him, Sky. We'll get him next time." Daxton said as he smiled.

Skyler wanted to know how long she had been out and told her parents that she had been able to hear the ocean and see the clouds. She tried to get up, but Kelsey pushed her back down. "Relax baby, just for a little bit. You've been out for about twenty minutes. You have no idea how worried we were. We love you so much and it seemed like forever." Kelsey told her.

"I'm okay Mom. Dad said I'm going to be okay so it's all good." She winked at Daxton and Kelsey just shook her head.

"Yes, baby, you are going to be okay. Please drink some water and I will let you sit up slowly." Kelsey said using her nurse's soothing voice.

Mateo got up to give Daxton, Kelsey, and Skyler some time alone now that he knew Skyler was doing better. He walked over to Scott and motioned for him to walk off a little further from them.

"What's going on Mateo? You okay? Scott questioned.

Mateo pulled out his GPS and looked down at the screen telling Scott," I don't want to be insensitive about this situation, but we need to retrieve the case as soon as possible. Mark has ways to locate us. I'm sure of it. Just the fact that no one is guarding the island, or the submarine perplexes me. I think you and I need to go retrieve the case and let them get Skyler back down to the boat. The anti-venom seems to be working but she should not be exerting herself any more than necessary."

Scott looked back at the three of them on the rock. "I agree Mateo. How long do you think we have left to reach it?"

Mateo looked up the hill and then back at the GPS. "I'm going to say no more than an hour up and back."

Scott let his eyes measure the distance they had come and the distance up the hill. "Okay, let's go tell them the plane and get moving!"

Scott and Mateo returned to Daxton, Kelsey, and Skyler and kneeled next to them. "Look guys, Mateo and I are going to retrieve the case and we will meet you back at the boat."

Skyler sat up. "No! I'll be okay. I promise!" she said as she got dizzy and laid back down.

"Negative, Sky," Daxton told her. Then he said to Scott and Mateo "That will work guys. We'll let her rest for a few more minutes then start making our way back down to the boat. Sound okay to you ladies?" Kelsey and Skyler both shook their heads in agreement.

"Okay, you guys head out. We'll start making our way down shortly." Daxton told them. He looked off to the east and could see the storms starting to build. He had watched the weather and radar, but the storm was coming in faster than expected.

Kelsey saw his concern as he looked out over the ocean. "Are we going to be okay, Daxton? she asked. I'm getting tired of asking that question, but it just gets deeper and deeper with things here on every turn."

Daxton slung Skyler's pack over the frontside of his chest and then put his on his back as he said to Skyler, "Sky, how ya' feeling baby? Think you're ready to make your way back down the hill?"

"Yes, I'm ready Dad, I can make it," she told Daxton.

Kelsey and Daxton got on each side of Skyler and locked arms with her as she slowly stood. Kelsey took a quick look at where the snake had bitten her, and Daxton noticed the concerned look on her face. The wound was red, swollen, and puffy. Kelsey looked back at Daxton and shook her head back and forth. "We need to get to the boat and get your wound cleaned up Skyler".

Skyler asked, "Does it look bad Mom?" "It's fine Sky, I just want to clean it well, so you don't get an infection, that's all," Kelsey responded.

As they slowly began making their way back down to the boat Daxton turned and looked up at the jungle-covered hill. He could see Mateo and Scott about to crest the top ridge.

Scott started climbing the large rock that sat at the summit of the hill. "Stay here and I'll give you a hand up". He made it up the rock and then reached down for Mateo's hand as

Mateo reached up. They sat for a moment on the rock before they continued.

Mateo stared directly at Scott and asked, "Who are you working for?"

Scott looked back at him. "I worked for Liam Costano but no one now."

"You and I know that's not the truth Scott. I have a feeling I know the answer. I just need to confirm that you're on the right side of this operation." Mateo let him know that he was unsure.

Scott was quiet as he stood up. He could see the island and the ocean below him when his eye caught the storm that had been brewing off to the east and he said, "Mateo, we need to leave now."

"You didn't answer my question. We can stay here until you tell me the truth Scott" was Mateo's reply.

Scott stared off at the storm. "I can't tell you who I'm with Mateo, but I can tell you that I'm on your side as well as Daxton and Kelsey's. Can you understand and accept that?"

Mateo thought about the things Scott had done to help before telling Scott, "It seems you leave me no choice and that will have to do. You have been a friend to me and to them so I will trust you unless you give me a reason not to."

Scott shook his head in understanding as they both jumped down from the rock and continued their way down the other side of the hill. They were closing in on the case and within a few minutes it would be in their possession.

The storm to the east of them slowly sucked the heavy moisture deeper into the clouds. The winds became more turbulent, and the clouds became darker and darker.

Daxton also watched it grow but little did he or the others know that this was not the only storm that would be coming down on them very soon.

CHAPTER THIRTY EIGHT

The light winds began to hit Palm Island as Scott and Mateo closed in on the location. Mateo looked down at his GPS.

"We're only about fifty yards away now. There will be a rock that's shaped like a square with one black corner placed in front of the case."

Scott looked at the trees that had started to sway with the winds. "We need to get it and get back down. This storm looks like it's getting a little bigger than we anticipated and it's forming right around us."

They kept moving down the hill until Mateo took another look at his GPS. "We're here, we are on top of it!" They both started scanning the area. Scott's eyes moved back and forth across the landscape. "Boom! There it is Mateo!" He pointed as he quickly proceeded to close in on the square rock.

Scott instructed Mateo to grab the side and help him lay the rock down. Mateo grabbed one side while Scott handled the other. Together they managed to pull the rock down to its face, it broke into a few large pieces. There were palm husks behind the rock that they both hurriedly began removing and throwing behind them. As Mateo reached deep into the husks he could feel the outline of the case. "It's here. Keep pulling that out."

Scott scrambled to pull all the remaining husks out as the winds became stronger.

Once they had removed all the husks they could see the case. They looked at each other and back at the case.

Mateo reached in grabbed the carbon fiber handle and dragged the case out of its temporary tomb.

"Okay, we've got it now, let's go, Mateo," Scott said.

Mateo shook his head. "I know you aren't going to want me to carry it if it makes it easier on you to get back down," he said as he looked at Scott then he looked back at the case. "Scott, I trust your word." And he handed Scott the case.

Mateo told him, "Besides, I'm getting this weird feeling that if I carry that it's going to be like that Indiana Jones thing where Nazis come from all sides."

Scott shook his head and said." Mateo, you watch too much TV!"

Daxton looked again up at the sky that had started to turn dark purple. "Dammit, this wasn't supposed to be happening yet!" He threw his and Skyler's backpacks up on the boat deck. "You good Sky? How are you feeling?"

She sat down on a log next to a large dark-colored rock.

Daxton came and knelt in front of her. He put his palms on each side of her head and kissed her on the forehead and as he did his eyes caught something on the rock. He went quiet, took his hands from Skyler's head, and walked around the dark rock. He stood there for a moment before he ran his hands over the chiseled markings imprinted into the rock.

"Dad, are you okay?" Skyler asked.

Daxton was silent as he stared at the markings. He slowly ran his hand over the grooves. The markings consisted of two lines in front and then a hook with an arrow on top of it.

"Kelsey, get a phone and let me get a picture of this." Kelsey reached into her pack and pulled her phone out, thankful that she had charged it while she was on the boat. She handed it to Daxton, and he stood back and took fifteen or twenty photos of the markings.

"What is it Daxton?" Kelsey asked as Daxton handed her phone back to her.

"I have no idea but it's not fresh. It's been here for a long while. Parks mentioned he was down here looking around the island before he got too much pressure from the local authorities."

His brain switched back to the current situation they found themselves in. "Okay, let's get all our stuff loaded in the boat. The guys should be headed back by now and we need to be ready to go when they get here," he told Kelsey and Skyler.

He took a quick glance up to the top of the hill. The trees were beginning to sway harder, and the wind was beginning to get cooler.

"Dad, what were those markings you were looking at? What do you think they could be?"

Daxton shrugged his shoulders. "I have no idea Sky. We will shoot it to Parks as soon as we get out of this mess."

As Skyler and Daxton were talking, Kelsey was standing ankle-deep on the shoreline with her back to them. She was looking over the ocean and her eyes were fixated on something heading their way.

"Kels, we need to get you loaded, You okay? Daxton asked her.

Kelsey was quiet for a few moments concentrating on what she was looking at and then she turned and looked back at Daxton. "I think we're about to have some company!"

Daxton threw one of the bags up into the boat and ran over to stand close to Kelsey. "What are you talking about Kelsey, company? "

"Look Dax, out there! Two boats. They're coming fast and heading this way." Kelsey answered.

Daxton climbed into the boat and flipped up the rear seat. "Dammit! How does anyone know we are out here?"

There were three old assault rifles and five extra clips for each of the weapons. Daxton grabbed one of the rifles and slammed the thirty-round magazine into the base. Then he retrieved the other two and slung them over his shoulder. He looked back at Kelsey and Skyler, and they could tell he was in serious mode. "They aren't coming to make peace; I can tell you that. No one flies in like that to bring you lunch and a margarita. I need you to get out of the boat Sky. You and your Mom need to get back behind those rocks up there on that second ledge. Like now, let's go!"

Skyler and Kelsey made their way off the boat. Kelsey took hold of Skyler's hand and they headed to the ridge.

Daxton pulled his small set of binoculars out of a bag and rested his elbows on the front of the boat. He spun the focus wheel on top of the binoculars and the boats started to come into focus. "Fuck, not good!" Daxton could see two boats and what looked like four to five men on each boat. All of them were armed and wore tactical gear. "Yeah, totally not good." He reached down and racked a round into the chamber. He looked back up and saw that Kelsey and Skyler were making their way around the second ledge where they dropped behind the rocks. He knew once he opened fire all hell would break loose on top of him, he also knew that eight fully automatic rifles vs. one half-rusted M1 did not put the odds in his favor. He looked back up the hill to see if he could catch a view of Scott and Mateo. "C'mon guys, where are you?" he muttered as he looked for cover. He knew he didn't want to head up the ledge as he wanted distance between them and Kelsey and Skyler. Daxton spotted a larger rock around fifty yards behind the boat. He carefully crouched and eased his way slowly to the rock. He was aware they had most likely already spotted him near the boat and probably had seen Kelsey and Skyler going up the hill.

He turned one more time and looked to see if Scott and Mateo were coming down. "Dammit!" Daxton whispered under his breath again. There was no sign of them. Daxton recognized the danger they were all in. They were extremely outgunned and outmanned, but they had a better chance of getting out of the situation if they were all together.

The two boats were closing in on the shoreline. As it slowed down one of the men aimed his weapon and opened fire on their small boat. Shots riddled the outboard engine and went through the hull. Another of the men raised his rifle and emptied his magazine into the boat.

They lit a Molotov cocktail and threw it onto the bullet-ridden boat. "You guys can all go ahead and come on out now! "He yelled.

Daxton analyzed what to do next, but he hesitated. Mark pointed up to the rocks ordering his men "Send a few rounds up to those rocks." Two of the men fired up at the rocks that Kelsey and Skyler were crouched behind.

Kelsey and Skyler held onto each other tightly. They could hear the bullets whiz by, and the rock chips flew into the air and rained back down on them.

Mark motioned for the men to stop and wait for any movement or response.

Daxton took a quick peek around the rock he was behind. He pulled back the slide to check the round. He took a deep breath and stood up with his rifles aimed. As soon as he popped up the men all opened fire. He threw his body back to the ground and covered his head. What seemed like one hundred rounds flew toward him into the rock and all over the beach. Daxton decided he had to try and talk this one out. He had no idea how it would go but he had zero options left if he wanted a chance to get his family off the island alive. The gunfire stopped and Daxton yelled over the rock," Alright, Alright I get the point. If I come out, can you hold your fire for just a minute? Jesus!"

"Yeah, sure, c'mon out, and let's see if we can work this out. Mark spun his gun into the air and rolled his eyes. "I got this one guys. Hold your fire."

Skyler heard a rock fall from further up the hill and looked behind her in the direction of the noise. Scott was crouched down behind a large tree and a set of rocks and vines. He held his pointer finger up to his lips signaling them to be quiet. Skyler poked Kelsey and pointed up at Scott. He motioned for them to lie down, and he disappeared back into the foliage.

Scott moved closer to Mateo who was already in position. Mateo's head was bleeding from getting hit in the head by a guard's stock as they were ambushed retrieving the case. "Sorry, I couldn't get to both of them faster Mateo. You good?"

"Yes, you saved my life and ripped those guys to pieces. Seriously, who the hell are you?" Mateo asked again.

Scott put his rifle into position and scanned the men telling Mateo "Work your way from the outside men toward the center. I'm going to fire on Mark first. One three, you ready?"

Mateo closed one eye and fixed his sights on the man furthest on the left. He shook his head indicating yes, he was ready.

At the same time, Daxton slowly began to stand up with his hands in the air. The men all turned and took aim at Daxton.

It was at that moment that Scott started counting down and everything seemed to happen in slow motion. 3....2....1...

Both Scott and Mateo started squeezing off rounds. Scott's first round struck Mark in the upper chest, and he spun around and hit the sand. Mateo's first round struck the outside guard in the neck. The guard shot rounds everywhere as he fell to his knees and blood poured from his wound.

Daxton dropped back behind the rock to grab his weapon. He rolled out from behind the rock and opened fire on the other guards. Two more guards hit the sand and the tables were starting to turn. Daxton dropped another and he fired two more rounds into the guard's body after he fell to the ground. Mark was dragging his way back over the side of the boat as others were shooting it out like the Old West. Blood smeared along the fiberglass as he threw his pistol into the boat.

Scott took a deep breath and steadied his rifle. He was fixated on one of the guards hiding behind a rock that was just a little too small to fully protect him. He placed his finger on the trigger and squeezed. The bullet found its way into the part of the guard's upper head that was barely exposed. His head exploded and his body lay limp as blood oozed into the sand.

"Three more mother fuckers! C'mon out."

All Daxton could think about was Kelsey and Skyler huddled up behind that group of rocks. "Hey boss, you good?" Scott yelled as he made his way down the ridge moving from cover spot to cover spot. Two guards fired up into the jungle and then over toward Daxton.

"All good, you guys good? Kelsey y'all good?" Daxton screamed up the hill.

"We're good Dax!" her voice quivered but she managed to scream back.

"Good boss, let's clean this up and go home." Scott continued laying down fire at the two guards that were left. Mateo managed to hit one of the guards in the arm. The tree that he was hiding behind didn't cover him well and his arm was exposed.

As he watched the guard closely, he noticed the glass door on the back of the boat slide open slowly. There stood Mateo's wife with Mark holding a pistol to the back of her head. Mateo's heart stopped and he yelled at the others. "Hold your fire! Hold your fire! He has my family on that boat!"

Daxton pointed his rifle at Mark, but he was too far away, and Daxton wasn't in any way confident that his open sights and forty-year-old rifle could make that precision shot. "Fuck!" Daxton said as he held his rifle up.

Mark put his pistol into the air and fired a shot and then held it to Mateo's wife's ear yelling angrily "Okay, I'm completely done with this now! Bring that case to the fucking boat or she has five seconds before I kill her Mateo!"

"Okay! Stop! Stop! It's right up there. I will bring it. Mateo shuffled around the rocks and held the case in the air. "It's right here! I'm coming down."

Scott slowly followed Mateo closely as he made his way down the hill with the case. As Mateo got closer to the beach the door to the boat slid open and his oldest son, afraid for his mother's life, came running out and started hitting Mark. Mark spun around and hit him on the bridge of the nose with his pistol.

"Nooooo! He's thirteen years old you piece of shit! Let him be!" Mateo's wife screamed and cried trying to go to her son's aid. Mark fired another shot into the air and drug her back with the collar of her shirt. He once again placed the pistol against her head and Mateo fell to his knees begging "Please let them go! They have done nothing, nothing!"

"Oh, but you have Mateo and I warned you this would happen if you didn't stick with the plan. He fired a shot into the sand near Mateo. Mark stood slightly behind Mateo's wife, not allowing Scott or Daxton to get in a clear shot.

"Everybody lay those guns down now! The games are over. Bring me the damn case! I will throw your family off the boat when I leave here." Mark said.

Mateo continued toward the boat holding the case in front of him.

CHAPTER THIRTY NINE

Mateo inched closer and closer to the boat now holding the case above his head. He slowly waded into the knee-deep water where he stood only feet from Mark and his wife. Mateo's wife looked into his eyes in absolute terror. He could see his son bleeding on the back deck of the boat. Mateo trudged through the water and thrust the case over onto the back deck of the boat. "There! There they are. Everything is in there!"

Mark just smiled at Mateo. 'Well, that's just superb now, isn't it? And now I want you to watch your wife die Mateo.

I never broke a promise, and I promised you this would happen. Tell her goodbye Mateo."

Mark pulled his pistol into place and began to squeeze the trigger, the hammer slowly started to come back as a loud crack came from the top of the jungle-covered hill. The .338 Lapua round struck Mark right above his eye at nearly three thousand feet per second. The top of his head exploded with skull fragments and brain matter splattering the back of the boat.

His limp body hit the deck of the boat and his blood poured onto the white fiberglass.

Mateo's wife screamed in shock, but she instantly ran to come to the aid of their son who held his bleeding face. Mateo jumped into the boat and ran to check on their other children.

Scott and Daxton both looked up the hill trying to see where the shot had come from.

"That shot came from the top of that hill. Everybody stays down!" Daxton yelled at the group. They heard the noise before they saw them. Four large black helicopters came forcefully flying over the ridge.

"What in the……" Daxton said as the helicopters got into position to land. They slowly settled into the sand as debris swirled around them from the turbulence they created.

Scott walked calmly over to Daxton and reached his hand down to pull him off the ground. "They are with me, boss. They're on our side. Go get your family. Daxton looked perplexed as he turned and ran up the ridge toward Kelsey and Skyler.

He rounded the corner and held onto them both. "Are you okay? I love you so much! It's over!"

Kelsey reached around Daxton's neck, kissed him on the lips, and said, "We want to go home, Dax. Please take us home."

Daxton hugged Skyler tightly, "You doin' okay kiddo?"

"Yeah, I'm okay Dad. That was easier than getting hit by a Mamba, just sayin". Skyler said.

Daxton shook his head, understanding that was Skyler's way of releasing stress from the situation they had endured.

Kelsey's eyes widened as a man in a Ghile suit slowly walked up behind Daxton. Daxton spun around and the man slipped off the head portion of his suit. telling them," You're all safe now. Why don't we all head down with the others and let's get you checked out and off this island."

As they followed the sniper down the ridge, the group watched as four boats appeared from around the side of the island. Men poured out of the helicopters onto the sandy beach and secured the area.

At the same time Daxton, Kelsey, and Skyler reached the beach the helicopter blades slowed to a stop. Scott stood in the sand speaking to a man dressed in a collared shirt and tie. He wore dark sunglasses and had his tactile boots tucked into his dress slacks. As Daxton walked up to the men he turned and stuck his hand out to shake it.

"Mr. Daxton Shaw, Scott here has told me all about you and your family. I want to apologize for being a bit late to the party. My name is Agent Thomas and I represent the External Special Ops Division."

Daxton looked perplexed at the man and then looked at Scott, so Agent Thomas said to Scott "Why don't you go fill Daxton in and I'll go survey the damage. "I will have medics check out your family and assist them in any way we can.

Kelsey watched as Agent Thomas's men helped pull Mateo's family safely off the boat and onto the beach. A medic immediately began assessing Mateo's son and began cleaning and treating his son's facial laceration as his mother sat beside him, a blanket covering her shoulders.

As Daxton walked with Scott he checked on Kelsey and Skyler. "I need a minute with Scott, but I won't be far if you need me," he told them.

Daxton and Scott walked away from the group, and he remained quiet.

"Daxton, I work for the External Ops Division. I've been working on and tracking this since we intercepted information about its existence. It's been almost two years. I want to say this changes nothing. I came to love your wife and daughter like my own family while I worked for Liam. I protected them as I worked on this project and tried to keep them out of harm's way. Then you were introduced to me and became my friend almost immediately. There is so much to talk about but for now, I want you to know this changes nothing. I will always be your friend and a protector of your family. I hope you can understand Daxton."

Daxton sat silently on a rock. He looked down at the ground and shook his head. After a few seconds, he looked up at Scott slowly.

"You just called me Daxton you son of a bitch! I think I like boss way better!" Daxton stood up and bear-hugged Scott. "Thank you, Scott, we have all reported to someone at some point in our lives. Thank you for being there for them. Thank you for being there for all of us. And yeah, we have some talking to do." Daxton smiled at Scott as they walked back near the choppers. Scott knew that if anyone understood it would be Daxton.

Daxton and Scott walked to where Kelsey and Skyler were both being checked out by the medics.

"It's okay Kels. We're all safe," he told her. He looked back as Mateo and his family were being loaded onto one of the boats. "Where are they taking them, Scott?" "They are taking them to a safe location until they can be placed into a protection program." was the unexpected answer that Daxton received.

"What do you mean? We won't see Mateo again?" Daxton asked. "Unfortunately, Daxton probably not," Scott said.

Mateo turned around and looked in their direction. The boat started up and began to move and as the boat left the beach area Mateo waved. They waved back to him as the boat slowly made its way from the island.

Scott pointed to one of the choppers in the back telling them, "Alright guys, that's our ride out of here. They will be here a little longer picking up the pieces and cleaning up this mess. Let's go."

Agent Thomas hurried over to Daxton and Scott, "Mr. Shaw, once you all get rested and make it back, we will sit. We have some things to talk about but for now, relax and enjoy the ride."

Scott grabbed Kelsey's hand and helped her into the helicopter followed by Skyler. Daxton jumped in behind them and soon they were all belted.

The engine fired up Daxton and watched out the window as men picked up shell casings, tossing pieces of debris into the boat, and raking back the island. They worked in unison, and he knew it wasn't their first rodeo.

As the sand began to spin into the air the helicopter slowly lifted. Kelsey reached for Skyler and Daxton's hands. The helicopter did one pass around the immediate area and Palm Island slowly disappeared as they made their journey across the ocean.

CHAPTER FOURTY

The helicopter abruptly landed on the pavement at the military base. Skyler had been sleeping but the jarring woke her up.

Kelsey reached over and pushed the hair away from Skyler's eyes. "We've landed baby." She tried to whisper in her ear over the engine noise. The engines shut down and the blades slowly came to a slow rotation.

Scott tapped Daxton on the knee and waved his head toward the door of the aircraft. They were all unbuckled and one by one they exited onto the hot asphalt. Scott motioned for them to follow him toward the hangar where a Leer jet sat with the side stairs down. Scott turned and looked at Daxton. "This is where the journey ends for me, my friend. That plane will take you and your family to a safe place until we can explain the situation and make sure you are out of harm's way for a time."

Daxton, as quick-witted as he was, could think of nothing to say at that moment.

"You promise me, my family and I will be safe if we get on that plane. Are you saying that we will not see you again, Scott?"

"Trust me you are safe now, follow their guidance, and don't worry about a thing. As far as seeing me again, I can't give you an answer now, but I would like to say it's not goodbye, but I will see you all soon," Scott promised.

Kelsey ran over and hugged Scott like he had never been hugged. She held onto him for almost a minute then pushed herself back. She kissed him on the cheek. "I can never repay you for what you have done for my family. Thank you and please come back to us."

Skyler ran over as well and gave him another long hug telling him, "I'm going to miss you. And you aren't as tough as you look! She looked up at Scott and could see tears forming in the overgrown man's eyes. She wiped them away, hugged him one more time, and went to her Mom's side.

Daxton went to Scott and looked him in the eyes. Scott hugged Daxton while he patted his back. "You take care of your family Daxton Shaw. Never lose them again or I will come and find your ass."

Daxton stepped back. "I cannot thank you enough, so I won't. And you're right, this isn't goodbye. You just asked me to take care of my family and never lose them again. Well, you are part of our family now so get your things in order here and come find us big guy!" Daxton winked at Scott, turned around, and grabbed Kelsey and Skyler around the neck. He kissed them on the side of their heads as they made their way into the jet with their destination unknown.

CHAPTER FOURTY ONE

Three and a half months later: Undisclosed Island. Daxton pushed the button on the blender and the colorful fresh fruit contents blended making the perfect breakfast. He poured the contents into two cups and headed out the back door as Jack Johnson played softly in the background.

Skyler was on the beach throwing a piece of driftwood to a dog that she had taken in recently. Daxton held up the drinks.

"Hey Sky, time for breakfast!" Daxton walked over to the hammock where Kelsey lay reading her book.

"Hey handsome, is that for me?" Kelsey said playfully.

"Yes, ma'am it sure is but you know it's gonna cost you." Daxton winked.

Kelsey smiled and pursed her lips. Daxton bent over kissed her lips and handed her breakfast. She took a big sip from the cup, "Thank you, my love, I don't think I will ever get over how good the fruit is down here." she told Daxton.

Skyler ran over and Daxton handed her a cup. He gave her a kiss on the forehead and asked, "Did you get some sleep sweetheart?" She shook her head yes as she downed the drink. "I did but the freaking monkeys woke me up at like five, so I went for a run."

Daxton shook his head. "Thanks for waiting for us!" he teased. "What do you guys think about doing a little spearfishing this morning and maybe walking up to town later in the afternoon? We can grab some things to cook up some fish tacos?"

Skyler smiled, "You know I'm in!"

Kelsey shook her head affirmatively. "Let me get us a bag packed Dax. Can I at least finish breakfast?" she said smiling.She winked at him as she pulled herself out of the hammock. At the same time, Skyler noticed a man walking beside the house in their direction. He was dressed in shorts and a button-up Hawaiian shirt and wearing dark glasses.

"Dad, we have company!" Skyler pointed in the direction of the visitor.

Daxton made his way around the hammock and placed himself in between Skyler, Kelsey, and their guest. "Good morning, can I help you with something?" The man walked closer and asked "Daxton Shaw?"

"Haven't seen that guy in over a few months. What can I do for you? "The man was now standing in front of Daxton.

"I have a letter for you," he said as he handed Daxton a small sealed manilla envelope.

Kelsey and Skyler came closer to Daxton as he opened the envelope and slid the handwritten letter out.

The letter read:

Family,

I hope you have settled in nicely and caught up on some well-deserved rest. In forty-eight hours, we will activate and meet in an undisclosed location. Please have your things in order and be ready to go.

The Big Guy…...

Daxton smirked. "It's Scott Dad!" Skyler said as she grabbed the letter and read it again. The man nodded his head. "You guys go and have yourself a good day now okay." He slowly turned and walked away the same way he came.

Daxton watched him walk away. "Well, guys looks like we need to go hit the water and get back. Sounds like we have some packing to do."

Acknowledgments

I would like to thank my amazing wife April for giving me the push to start writing more again, for being supportive, listening to my ideas, and assisting me in following my dreams. Our travels, life, and adventures together have inspired me on so many levels. Thank you for always being there and for doing life with me. And to my wonderful kids who continue to drive and inspire me daily.

I would also like to thank my parents for always being in my corner and having my back. To my mother for listening to my ideas, helping edit, and giving honest feedback on my writing. To my buddy Todd Rodgers for pushing me into this crazy writing world.

And to all the people we have met along the way in our travels and experiences. Each of these memories gained along the way usually will appear within one of my stories.

Jason L. Bradshaw Biography:

Jason Bradshaw has had a passion for adventure, history and writing for most all of his life. This is what led him to write his first novel "Beneath Creek Waters" which was published in 2014 that takes place in a small Texas creek. He went on to write the second novel of the series "Beneath Gulf Waters" in 2021. Jason has also written numerous articles for various newsletters and publications. Jason has co-written two full action screenplays with writer and director Todd Rodgers by the titles of "Red Eye" and "Shadow Ops."

Jason currently resides on the south Texas coastal bend with his wife April and their four children. He continues to write and explore the world with his wife.

Jason has shipped multiple boxes of books to our wonderful men and woman of the military. He fully supports those that protect our freedom and loves to share the joy and adventure of reading with those that are away from their families while they put their lives on the line.

Made in the USA
Columbia, SC
11 August 2024

478e815f-97c8-4e64-9fae-55cfb2d786dfR02